ST. NORBERT COLLEGE
309.26097468 P27b
Patterns of urban ch
3 5109 0004 8758 5

Patterns of Urban Change

Patterns of Urban Change

The New Haven Experience

David Birch
Reilly Atkinson
Sven Sandström
Linda Stack

Lexington Books
D.C. Heath and Company
Lexington, Massachusetts
Toronto London

Library of Congress Cataloging in Publication Data

Main entry under title:

Patterns of urban change.

1. Regional planning–New Haven metropolitan area. 2. Cities and towns–Planning–New Haven. 3. Cities and towns–Planning–Mathematical models. I. Birch, David L.
HT394.N47P3 309.2'62'097468 73-18296
ISBN 0-669-90951-3

Published simultaneously in Canada.

Printed in the United States of America.

International Standard Book Number: 0-669-90951-3

Library of Congress Catalog Card Number: 73-18296

Contents

List of Figures

List of Tables

Preface

This book is part of a fairly extensive research project conducted at the Harvard Graduate School of Business Administration over a period of several years. The project was initiated to develop methods and approaches for helping managers of organizations cope with the increasing complexity of the environment (in the general sense) in which they function.

The book does not provide the kind of mathematical detail another urban analyst would require in order to replicate our work. That is provided in a more extensive and technically-oriented volume entitled *The New Haven Laboratory.* Nor does the book provide the details of how a manager might translate the results of our findings into practical terms for his organization. That is the subject of a subsequent publication, not yet written. The applications research is already well underway, however, and some of the preliminary findings are mentioned briefly in Chapter 8. This book *is* designed for the non-technical, lay reader who is interested in how urban areas seem to function and change and who shares our interest in the consequences of the changes.

In a project lasting this long, the authors become indebted to numerous individuals who have provided data or technical assistance or financial assistance, or friendly advice, or all four.

Due to the strong empirical leanings of our work we have required (and collected) a substantial body of data. Without the continued willingness of such people as Norris Andrews of the Regional Planning Agency of South Central Connecticut, or David Holmes of the New Haven City Plan Department, or William Messner and Edward Bates of the Connecticut State Highway Department, or Harold Burdo of the Connecticut Health Department, we would never have been able to function. We are particularly indebted to the U.S. Census Bureau and all the people there who have cooperated with our efforts to obtain the kind of detailed, small-area information that has not been readily available in the past. Howard Brunsman, Caby Smith, George Leyland, Marshall Turner, and others have responded time and again to our requests.

Keeping a project of this sort afloat financially has been no small task. As the immediate purposes have changed, so have the funding sources. Much of the data preparation was funded by the U.S. Department of Commerce. The MIT-Harvard Cambridge Project provided generous support over several years to enable us to develop the new methods required to process and understand our data. The U.S. Department of Housing and Urban Development was the principal supporter of our modeling work over a two-year period. Application of the model in New Haven is now being financed by the National Science Foundation. The model's application in Houston, Texas, is supported by a planning grant from H.U.D. to the Houston/Galveston Area Council.

The Harvard Business School Division of Research has supported, and to a great extent guided, the project throughout its existence. The Division never hesitated to provide its own funds to fill the valleys between outside grants. We are particularly indebted to Lawrence Fouraker, Richard Walton, and James Baughman for insuring continuity over an extended period of time. We are indebted also to Bernard Frieden, who has provided an invaluable sounding board for many of our ideas at the MIT-Harvard Joint Center for Urban Studies, and to The Boeing Company for encouraging one of the authors to continue his work on the project while a Boeing employee.

Technically, our efforts were enhanced by the early involvement of Paul Teplitz, Howard Pifer, Nathan Dickmeyer, and Joseph Mooney. The typing of the endless manuscripts associated with this and other publications has been painstakingly and cheerfully undertaken by Susan Ufer, without whom we would never have completed our work. Susan was helped on occasion by Janis Daisey, and we are grateful to her as well.

Like Rabbit in *Winnie The Pooh,* with his many friends and relations, we have benefited continuously from the friendly advice of a number of people who, at one point or another, have reviewed our work and thereby helped to shape its course. In this potentially endless list must certainly be included Peter Allaman, Howard Christy, Wyndom Clarke, Richard Coleman, Samuel Colwell, Aaron Fleisher, Cyrus Gibson, James Glauthier, John Glover, Max Hall, Karla O'Brien, Joe Pyle, Arnold Rom, David Sawyer, and Raymond Vernon. In a special category–under the heading "relations"–fall our respective wives and husbands,–Louisa, Allegra, Erlinda, and Tom–who have willingly tolerated our romance with the PDP-10, and the sometimes unreasonable hours and lives that it has demanded.

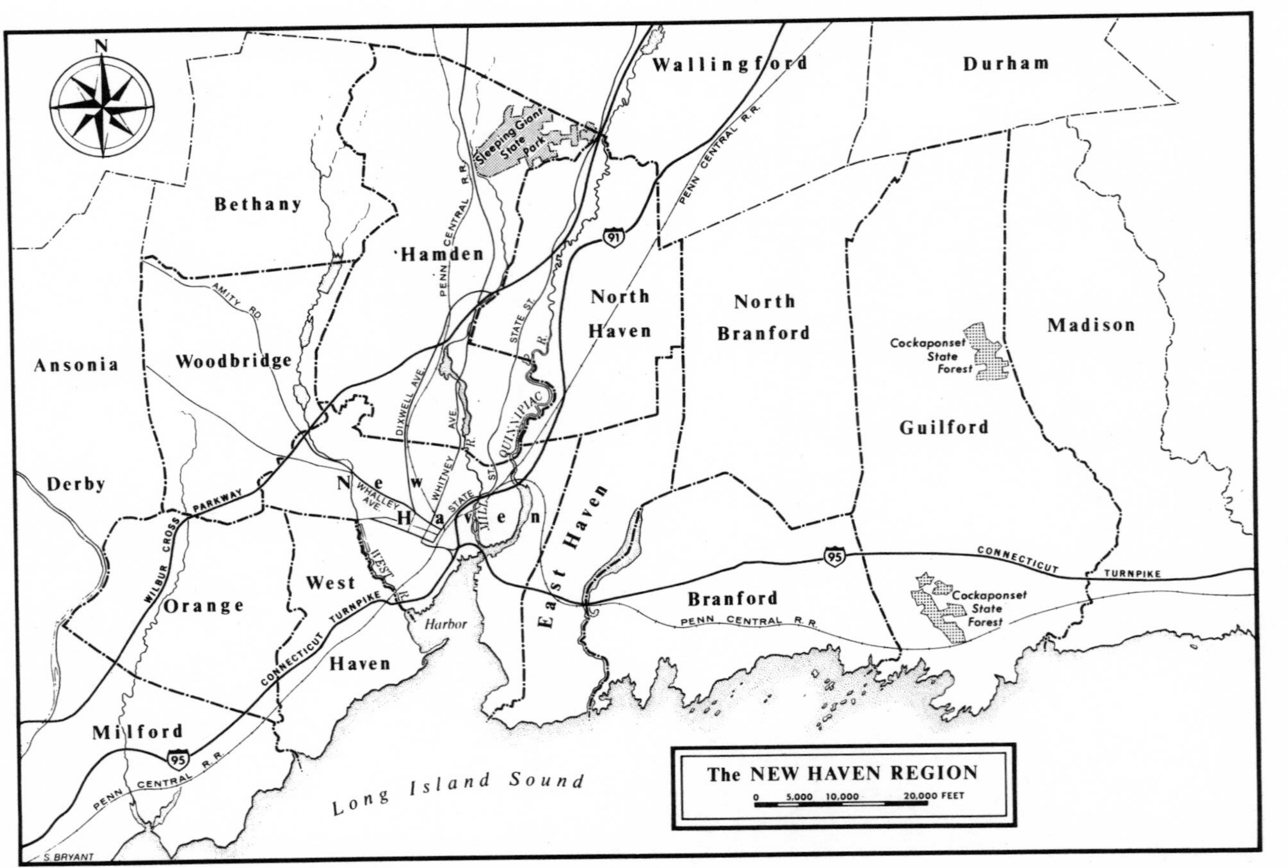
N
Durham
Wallingford
Bethany
Hamden
Sleeping Giant State Park
North Haven
North Branford
Madison
Cockaponset State Forest
Guilford
Ansonia
Woodbridge
Derby
New Haven
East Haven
West Haven
Orange
Milford
Branford
Cockaponset State Forest
Harbor
Long Island Sound
PENN CENTRAL R.R.
PENN CENTRAL R.R.
PENN CENTRAL R.R.
PENN CENTRAL R.R.
91
95
95
CONNECTICUT TURNPIKE
CONNECTICUT TURNPIKE
STATE ST.
STATE ST.
DIXWELL AVE.
WHITNEY AVE.
WHALLEY AVE.
AMITY RD.
WILBUR CROSS PARKWAY
QUINNIPIAC R.
MILL R.
WEST R.
S. BRYANT
The NEW HAVEN REGION
0 5,000 10,000 20,000 FEET

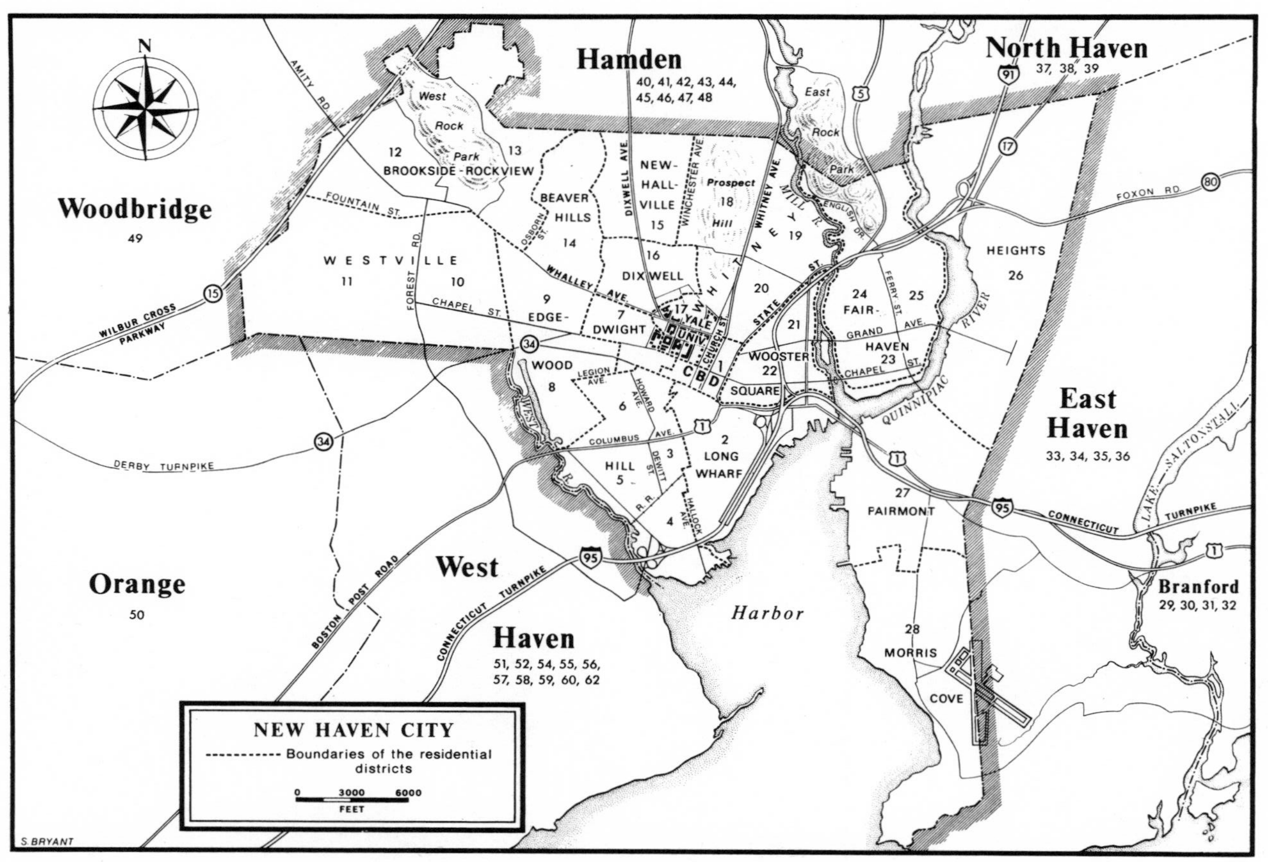
North Haven
37, 38, 39
Hamden
40, 41, 42, 43, 44,
45, 46, 47, 48
Woodbridge
49
Orange
50
West
Haven
51, 52, 54, 55, 56,
57, 58, 59, 60, 62
East
Haven
33, 34, 35, 36
Branford
29, 30, 31, 32
Harbor
West Rock Park
East Rock Park
12
13
BROOKSIDE - ROCKVIEW
BEAVER HILLS
14
NEW-HALL-VILLE
15
Prospect Hill
18
19
16
DIXWELL
WESTVILLE
11
10
9
EDGE-
7
DWIGHT
17
YALE
UNIV.
CBD
1
20
21
WOOSTER
22
SQUARE
24
FAIR-
25
HAVEN
23
HEIGHTS
26
WOOD
8
6
2
LONG
WHARF
3
HILL
5
4
27
FAIRMONT
28
MORRIS
COVE
FOUNTAIN ST.
FOREST RD.
CHAPEL ST.
WHALLEY AVE.
OSBORN ST.
DIXWELL AVE.
WINCHESTER AVE.
WHITNEY AVE.
STATE ST.
CHURCH ST.
LEGION AVE.
HOWARD AVE.
COLUMBUS AVE.
DEWITT ST.
HALLOCK AVE.
FERRY ST.
GRAND AVE.
ENGLISH DR.
FOXON RD.
AMITY RD.
WILBUR CROSS PARKWAY
DERBY TURNPIKE
BOSTON POST ROAD
CONNECTICUT TURNPIKE
MILL R.
QUINNIPIAC RIVER
WEST R.
LAKE SALTONSTALL
NEW HAVEN CITY
Boundaries of the residential districts
0 3000 6000
FEET
S.BRYANT

Patterns of Urban Change

1 The Context

For all the talk about the "Urban Crisis," and for all the courses in universities with the word "urban" in their titles, precious little is understood about how urban areas work. Many people have looked at one or another aspect of cities—the politics, the housing, the transportation, the demographics, the economics. Few have tried to understand how the parts combine to cause shifts in the whole. The purpose of this book is to offer an improved understanding of a few of the more important parts, to show how changes now taking place in the parts will affect the shape of the whole over the next decade or two, and to begin to suggest what the implications of such shifts might be for a broad range of managers and program designers.

The word "understand" is used in its strictest sense. That is, the person who truly understands a region should be able to predict its evolution accurately several years into the future at the neighborhood level. Much urban analysis falls by the wayside under this test. Yet it is the only test that is satisfactory to those who must formulate programs and make decisions, the success of which will depend upon the future course the region takes.

The price being paid for a poor understanding is going up each year. The days when the city could be viewed as a series of problems that could be solved by adjusting a relatively few "policy variables" are over. Attempt after attempt at doing just this sort of thing during the 1960's has failed. Well-intentioned programs have withered and died. Local administrators—public and private—have dug themselves into deeper and deeper holes in search of simple-minded solutions.

One of the causes of these difficulties has been the tendency of policy makers and administrators to act as though the things under their control are large relative to the system being fiddled with. The reality, of course, is that they are not. An urban region evolves as the result of millions of decisions made each year by hundreds of thousands of households. Only a few of these decisions are affected in any significant way directly by any single public or private action. The key to effective action in either sphere is first to understand—in the strict sense—the underlying dynamics that cause change, and then to enter at carefully chosen points with carefully chosen actions. By way of analogy, the region must be viewed in much the same way a large pendulum should be viewed by an energetic ant. Attempting to redirect the pendulum by standing in its way at the bottom of its swing would be foolhardy indeed for the ant. To deflect it at all, the ant must tap it at just the right place at just the right time; so too the administrator and program designer. They must understand the pressures causing change in detail and deflect rather than arrest those pressures if they are to have any lasting effect.

This book takes a step in the direction of understanding the underlying dynamics in some detail. We have chosen to focus our efforts on one relatively small area–New Haven, Connecticut[a] and to go into it in some depth. We have looked at this region through the eyes of the person trying to get things done rather than through the eyes of a utopian conjuring up an ideal city. We are interested in reality, not myths and dreams.

Our approach has been quite different from related past efforts. Most have started with theories; we started with facts. Several years were devoted to gathering information about what has actually happened in New Haven. As the data began to accumulate, we developed instruments to reveal patterns in the data and ultimately suggest explanations (or theories) of what was taking place. What emerged was an increasingly well-defined set of theories that explained how the "pieces" worked and how they fit together. As the theories took shape, they were "mounted" on a "frame" where they could be related easily to one another–the result being a computer simulation model of the region that can reproduce past history and make predictions for the future for each neighborhood in New Haven.

In our view, the computer model should be treated like a cake pan in a bakery. It is an essential tool for getting the job done, but it is not the end product. The thing that gets put on the shelf is the cake. This book will be about the cake, not about the pan. We will focus most of our attention on what we have learned about New Haven, and not how we got there. Most of our chapters will be about the behavior of people as individuals and members of households, and as builders, real estate agents, landlords, businessmen, workers, homeowners, and zoning board members. Then we will show how the pieces interact and, in the process, cause the region to change over time, and we will suggest some of the implications for administrators and program designers. For those of a technical bent, an appendix provides a brief introduction to the simulation model itself and will guide the reader to the appropriate source for a more detailed description.

It is our intention to make this book understandable and, we hope, interesting to the lay reader. We have tried not to hide behind equations and variable descriptions but to present only the essence, and the limitations, of what we have been able to observe thus far.

---

[a]Throughout this book, the New Haven region is defined as the 1960 Standard Metropolitan Statistical Area (SMSA); that is, the central city of New Haven and the eight surrounding towns of Guilford, Branford, East Haven, North Haven, Hamden, Woodbridge, Orange, and West Haven.

2 Three Hundred Thirty-Two Years of Evolution

The period we will be examining in great detail—the 1960's and the 1970's—is like a short interval on a long trajectory. New Haven has gone through several stages of evolution since its founding as a colony in 1638, each in response to a different set of stimuli. A close look at the tail end of that trajectory suggests that the stimuli are changing once again and that the future will not be like the past. The purpose of this chapter is to trace briefly the history of stimuli and responses to give the reader some feeling for urban structure and change at a macroscopic level before delving into detail.

Roughly speaking, New Haven spent 150 years getting organized and 150 years growing. More precisely, the 322 years from 1638 to 1960 break naturally into three periods: getting settled (1638 to 1800), industrial expansion (1800 to 1910), and integration as a region (1910 to 1960). Some evidence suggests that around 1960 a fourth phase began.

Getting Settled[a]

The original colony at Qunnipiack (renamed New Haven in 1640) was settled in 1638 under the leadership of a businessman (Theophilus Eaton) and a clergyman with strong educational leanings (John Davenport). They set a tone that persisted: a strong interest in commercial matters coupled with a desire for education, religious tolerance (the New Haven *Register* labeled New Haven "the city of Churches" in 1855), and a strong sense of civic pride.

It took New Haven a long time to get itself organized. Early attempts at remaining an independent colony collapsed in 1665 when New Haven was forced to join the Connecticut colony. Much energy was consumed during those first 150 years laying out streets, building buildings, developing the port as a center of economic activity, and setting up a stable political structure. Yale was founded in 1701. New Haven was constantly involved in turmoil with the British, sheltering, at one point, the three judges (Walley, Goeff, and Dixwell) who had signed the death warrant for King Charles I and fled England when his son Charles II was restored to the throne.

During the Revolution, the city was invaded and occupied for one day, the

[a]Much of the historical material in this chapter has been drawn from an extensive history of New Haven written by Rollin Osterweis [1].

only direct experience it has had with military violence. Nevertheless, New Haven played an active role in restructuring the colonies after the war, sending Roger Sherman to help formulate and to sign the "Articles of Association," the Declaration of Independence, the Articles of Confederation, and the Constitution of the United States. He was the only man to sign all four documents.

By 1784 when the City of New Haven received its official charter from the State of Connecticut, 3,350 people lived in about 400 houses occupying 10 percent of the land area assigned to the original New Haven colony. The surrounding towns claimed an additional 4,600 people. These towns (Guilford, Branford, East Haven, North Haven, Hamden, Woodbridge, Orange, and West Haven) received independent charters and operated largely as independent entities until the 20th century, a unique characteristic of New England regions. Other colonies relied far more heavily upon the county as the basic unit of government.

New Haven had its ups and downs economically. Several early ventures ended in disaster. Attention focused primarily on the port and the trading that went with it. In 1774, a large proportion (as high as 40 percent or 50 percent) of the able-bodied men were sailors. There were no factories to speak of prior to the Revolutionary War, just shops (57 of them in 1784). The war brought the first of the munitions plants (a gunpowder plant) that were to play a large role in New Haven's economy up to and including the Vietnam War. After the Revolution a few early plants for the manufacture of loaf sugar, cloth, and pennies were followed by another munitions venture—this one far more significant. In 1798, Eli Whitney built his Whitney Arms Plant to manufacture guns from interchangeable parts. He was the first of several successful entrepreneurs who were to turn New Haven into an industrial town during the next 100 years.

Industrial Expansion

Many of the factors traditionally cited by historians played a role in transforming New Haven from a seaport with an agricultural hinterland into a manufacturing center. The Embargo of 1808 (closing the port), the protective tariffs following the War of 1812, the steam-driven ship, and the growth of the South and the West as prosperous markets for manufactured goods—all entered into the picture. As Rollin Osterweis[b] points out in his history of New Haven, often overlooked by historians was the drive and skill and imagination of a number of businessmen who saw the newer opportunities and capitalized upon them.

One after another, these entrepreneurs matched a technology with a need and built a factory to bring the two together. Eli Whitney began with his gun plant,

---

[b]See Osterweis [1].

introducing the concept of interchangeable parts. He was later eclipsed by Oliver Winchester with his Winchester Repeating Arms Company, started in 1858. Through the efforts of John Cook, Jonathan Mix, and James Brewster, New Haven became a leading manufacturer of carriages, selling many of its coaches in the South. Thomas Nash made clocks. Charles Goodyear learned how to vulcanize rubber, and New Haven became a major producer of rubber products. Lewis Osterweis combined Connecticut outer leaves with Cuban tobacco to produce the "Connecticut-type" cigar. Issac Strouse and Max Adler joined to become the largest corset manufacturers in the world. Elisha Root manufactured some of the first machine tools.

The Civil War dried up the carriage market in the South. Of the 50 carriage shops that flourished in 1860, 21 remained in 1909. Other businesses rose to fill the gap, however, and the industrial growth continued unabated. Oliver Winchester built a larger plant in 1870. In that same year John Marlin established the Marlin Firearms Company. Joseph Sargent opened a hardware manufacturing plant; by 1865 it employed 2,000 persons. Nash's clock company expanded and prospered. By 1879 the *Register* reported that at least 3,000 people were employed in the manufacture of corsets. The cigar industry grew as well.

As the curves in Figure 2-1 suggest, after 150 years of getting organized, the 1800's were a period of very rapid growth. The industrial boom triggered two of the three waves of migration that populated the city and provided the labor force for the factories. The first wave started around 1830, consisting mostly of Irish and some Germans (the ratio was reputed to be five to one). These two groups and smaller clusters of others increased the population of the city from 11,000 in 1830 to 40,000 by 1860, making it the largest city in Connecticut—a position it maintained until 1920.

After the Civil War, the second wave came, slowly at first, and then rapidly during the 1800's and 1890's. This time it consisted of Italians and Jews, the latter coming mostly from Russia. By 1900 the population had risen to 108,000 and by 1910 it stood at 133,000. In 1910, the city fathers, extrapolating the experience of the past 40 years or so, estimated that the city might comfortably hold 400,000 people by 1950. At that very point, however, the dynamics of the urban growth process were changing underneath them in a way that they did not understand. Little did they know that the city had nearly reached its peak. Trees do not grow to the sky, and cities do not grow indefinitely. Had they looked carefully, they might have realized the consequences of the invention of the automobile. They would have observed the growing attraction of the outlying areas, accessible first through the horsedrawn trolley and later through the electric trolley and, ultimately, the car.

In all fairness though, it was difficult in the year 1910 to see the emergence of the suburbs as we now know them or the integration of the suburbs and the city into a region. Up to that time, most of the housing units constructed in the

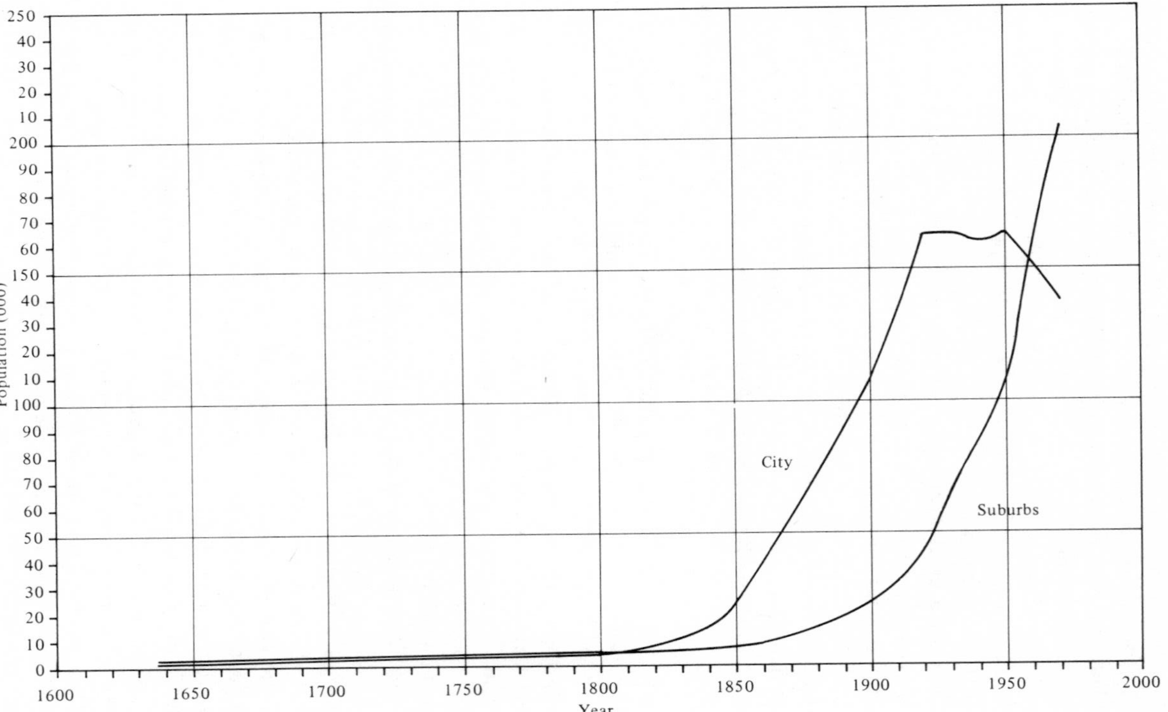

Source: U.S. Bureau of the Census [4] and Osterweis [1].

[a]All figures have been adjusted to correspond to the 1960 SMSA and central city boundaries.

Figure 2-1 Population of the Central City and Suburbs in the New Haven SMSA, 1638 to 1970

previous 100 years had been built to house the workers in the factories. The Hill, Newhallville, Dixwell, the area around State Street, and Fair Haven were filled with "triple deckers" to house the employees of Oliver Winchester and Joseph Sargent and James Brewster and Isaac Strauss and Max Adler. The plant owners were comfortably settled either in the center of town or on Prospect Hill in the Whitney Area. The maps at the beginning of the book show the location of these older New Haven neighborhoods.

The "outlying" communities of Westville and Beaver Hills and the Heights and Fairmont and Morris Cove were not even developed. The western half of Westville was a game preserve. Beaver Hills was farmland interspersed with a cemetery, a tennis club and a few houses. The Heights was an isolated, rural area and remained so until after World War II. Fairmont and Morris Cove were fashionable summer communities. The suburbs that we know today persisted in the tradition in which they were established in 1784—as independent settlements with very little travel back and forth to the city. The "suburban" population of 4,600 in 1784 had grown to only 31,000 by 1910 while the city proper jumped from 3,350 to 133,000. As Figure 2-1 illustrates so clearly, all this was to change over the next 60 years.

Integration of the Region

One obvious thing that stopped the population growth of the city dead in its tracks at 162,000 people from 1920 to 1950 was the automobile. In much the same manner that the horse-drawn trolley and the electric trolley opened up the "suburbs" of Westville, Beaver Hills, and Fair Haven, the automobile made West Haven, Woodbridge, Hamden, North Haven, The Heights, Fairmont, Morris Cove, East Haven, and eventually Orange and Branford and Guilford attractive residential options to the old center city. Prior to World War I, the suburban growth was almost entirely residential. After the war, stores and eventually factories moved out as well.

A more subtle cause of the change was the gradual obsolescence of the industries upon which the city had thrived for 100 years and the inability of the community to adapt to the new. Corsets and carriages and cigars were not the wave of the future. New Haven chose not to produce steel or electronics or oil or automobiles or airplanes. The city was sustained during the period from 1900 to 1950 primarily by inertia, the munitions booms of two wars, and the lack of change during the depression. From 1950 on, none of these forces was strong enough to hold people in the deteriorating dwellings that had been built in a previous century to house factory workers, and the exodus began.

The extent of the departure is, in fact, significantly understated by the total figures, for about this time a third wave of in-migration to the city compensated for much of the loss to the suburbs. This wave was black and, more recently,

Puerto Rican. New Haven has always had a black population. A small black community was described in the town records in 1646. It had grown to 200 by 1790 and 600 by 1820. One hundred years later it was still only 5,000 and by 1940 the figure stood at 7,000. World War II triggered the migration that started from the South. From 1940 through 1970, the region's black population has practically doubled every ten years, standing in 1970 at 50,000–roughly 15 percent of the region's total population of 332,000. There has been little apparent love between the white and black populations in recent years, and the entry of the one has surely served as a further stimulus to the out-movement of the other, a fact that will become quite clear in Chapter 4.

The striking thing about "suburbanization" of the outlying settlements has been its recentness. It had barely begun in 1920. In 1940, the city housed twice the population of all the suburbs combined. Around 1960 the city and the suburbs contained equal numbers of people; in 1970 the suburbs were over one and one-half times more populous and showed every sign of continuing their expansion. The cross-over around 1960 signaled a shift in the basic determinants and patterns of growth. It is at this point that we look at the city in detail.

The Decoupling of the Suburbs

A conspicuous fact of New Haven's history is that economics–particularly the economics associated with transportation–played a major role in determining the nature and speed and location of the region's growth. The city was founded on the economics of the port and trading. The city grew very little until the economics of the steam engine (as manifested in the steamboat and the railroad) opened up the South and the West as markets, and the economies of scale of mass production made it possible to meet the new demands. The location of growth within the region depended first on the horse, then the electric trolley, then the automobile.

A number of changes seem to be taking place, however, that reduce the relative significance of transportation as a determinant of growth. Access is no longer a major problem, either within the region or to others. It is now possible to reach almost any point in the region from any other point within the 35 minutes that most people seem willing to travel to get to work. The Interstate System and the expansion of air freight has put New Haven factories in touch with most parts of the country on an overnight basis, and thus reduced the importance of transportation as a determinant of industrial location within the region. Furthermore, manufacturing is declining as a source of employment while service and government job opportunities are expanding. Many of these newer kinds of jobs owe little or no debt to transportation and can be located anywhere.

The consequence of all this for the household seeking a new residence and the businessman seeking a new location is quite clear. For the first time in the history of the region, they can choose their spot as much on the basis of the social and physical environment in which they wish to live and work as on the economics of access. In particular, they can decouple themselves from the central city. The data in Table 2-1 suggest that, in fact, they are so doing. New Haven passed the point where over half the population is in the suburbs just prior to 1960. Suburban jobs have not yet reached the over-50 percent mark, but are clearly headed in that direction.

Of particular interest is the specialization that appears to be taking place in the central city. Manufacturing jobs are leaving New Haven city (or never entering it) at a rapid pace, as are jobs in construction, transportation, retail trade, and finance, insurance, and real estate. The city is holding its own, however, in communications, utilities, wholesale trade, services, and government. Fortunately for the city, service and government employment are two of the most rapidly expanding classes of employment in the nation as a whole, and in New Haven in particular. Central city growth in these two sectors was more than enough to compensate for the decline in the other categories, and total central city employment actually grew from 88,000 in 1960 to 93,000 in 1970.

The recent boom in downtown office space suggests, at least for New Haven, that the central city is becoming a service center for the region, acting as a collecting point for many of those activities that require a good deal of face-to-face communication, e.g., corporate headquarters, law offices, advertising firms, printers, utilities, commercial banks, government offices, hospitals, and so forth.

The suburbs, on the other hand, show every sign of creating independent

Table 2-1
Trends in the New Haven SMSA, 1960 to 1970[1]

	Central City		*Suburbs*		*Suburban Share*	
	1960	*1970*	*1960*	*1970*	*1960*	*1970*
Total Population	146,000	130,000	159,000	202,000	52%	61%
Minority	24,000	42,000	2,000	8,000	8%	15%
Total Occupied Housing Units	49,000	47,000	46,000	62,000	49%	57%
Total Employment	88,000	93,000	38,000	61,000	30%	40%
Manufacturing	29,000	17,000	16,000	25,000	35%	60%
Service and Gov't	24,000	37,000	8,000	14,000	25%	28%

Source: See Table 4-1

[1]Figures in this table refer to the SMSA as defined in 1960. Adjustments have been made to make the 1970 figures comparable. Population figures do not include people living in group quarters, i.e., students in dormitories, patients in hospitals and retirement homes, and so forth. Suburban percentage shares may disagree slightly with absolute numbers in the table due to rounding.

Table 2-2
Percent of Jobs Located in the Suburbs, Percent of Central City Workers who Live in the City and Work in the Suburbs, and Percent of Suburban Workers who Live and Work in the Suburbs for the 120 Largest U.S. Metropolitan Areas (SMSA's) in 1960 and 1970

	1960	*1970*
Percent of Jobs in the Suburbs		
Smaller SMSA's	34%	40%
Medium-sized SMSA's	38%	48%
Large SMSA's	36%	45%
Percent of Central City Workers Commuting to Suburban Jobs		
Smaller SMSA's	11%	17%
Medium-sized SMSA's	10%	20%
Large SMSA's	9%	14%
Percent of Suburban Workers Who Live and Work in the Suburbs		
Smaller SMSA's	60%	60%
Medium-sized SMSA's	64%	66%
Large SMSA's	68%	72%

Source: Derived from U.S. Bureau of the Census [2, 3]

Note: The sample included all SMSA's with over 250,000 people in 1970 that existed and had over 100,000 people in 1960. Jacksonville, Florida was omitted because of difficulties with the data for that region. No adjustments have been made for the annexation of suburban towns by central cities. Such annexation was prevalent in many southern and western communities during the 1960's. Ignoring annexation understates the extent of the suburban gain based on the 1960 boundaries.

SMSA's were ranked by size according to the number of workers rather than the number of people. The categories are: smaller (under 500,000), medium sized (500,000 to 1,000,000) and large (over 1,000,000).

Distribution of total jobs was estimated from jobs held by metropolitan workers. To the extent that the number of workers commuting out of the region each day is different from the number commuting in, the estimates will be inaccurate. In New Haven, for example, the estimates of suburban share are 30 percent and 42 percent for 1960 and 1970, and the actuals, drawn from a much richer data base (see Table 2-1), are 30 percent and 40 percent respectively.

living and working environments for most of their residents. Between 1960 and 1970, suburban population jumped 27 percent from 159,000 to 202,000 while suburban jobs jumped 61 percent from 38,000 to 61,000. The percentage of people who live in the suburbs and work in the suburbs rose from 46 percent in 1960 to 52 percent in 1970. The number of reverse commuters (those who live in the city and work outside) jumped from 14 percent of the central city work force in 1960 to 24 percent in 1970. In other words, almost a quarter of the workers who live in the city are now employed in the jobs that have sprung up in the suburbs. If past trends are any indication, many of these reverse commuters would prefer to live in the more attractive suburban settings and will move there when the opportunity arises.

In short, the suburbs (and the outlying towns beyond) are well on their way to regaining the degree of independence they enjoyed prior to the advent of the automobile. Their dependence upon the central city as a place of employment is dwindling. As in earlier days, for most people, the trip to the center need be made only a few times a year to see a banker or a circus or a government official.

As a consequence, the dynamics that will be affecting the patterns of growth in the future will be different than they have been for the past 100 years. As indicated earlier, releasing the constraints of access to work permits factors such as physical quality of neighborhood, good schools, proximity to recreational facilities, and "nice" neighbors to dominate the relocation process.

There is some evidence that the New Haven experience is not unique. Table 2-2 summarizes the recent experience of 120 of the largest metropolitan areas across the country, broken down by size. As can be seen from the table, the suburban share of jobs, the extent of out-commuting from the central city, and the percent of workers who live and work in the suburbs increased uniformly during the 1960's for all classes of regions, the larger SMSA's being farther advanced along these dimensions than the smaller ones in most cases. The point at which large numbers of metropolitan areas will have over half their jobs in the suburbs and will provide three-quarters of their suburban residents with suburban jobs is rapidly approaching. One purpose in collecting detailed data for New Haven since 1960 (and attempting to build a simulation model that would explain it) was to learn more of the nature of the forces that are producing this pattern.

References

1. Osterweis, Rollin G. *Three Centuries of New Haven.* New Haven: Yale University Press, 1953.

2. U.S. Bureau of the Census. *Census of Population: 1970, Detailed Characteristics.* Final Report PC(1)-D1, Washington, D.C. : U.S. Government Printing Office, 1973.

3. U.S. Bureau of the Census. *U.S. Census of Population: 1960, Characteristics of the Population.* Part 1, United States Summary, Washington, D.C.: U.S. Government Printing Office, 1964.

4. U.S. Bureau of the Census. *U.S. Census of Population: 1960, Selected Area Reports, Standard Metropolitan Statistical Areas.* Final Report PC(3)-1D, Washington, D.C.: U.S. Government Printing Office, 1963.

3 Approach

Our initial research questions centered not on a set of theories about regions, but on the needs of administrators trying to function in one. As we talked with bank presidents and city planners and manufacturers and school superintendents and utility executives in New Haven, it became clear that each one could do a better job of planning if he or she knew what the region would be like five and ten years in the future. Our initial question was: What properties must a projection of a region have in order to be useful to these people?

The administrator's first requirement was to have confidence in the method. This meant, in particular, that any approach we used had to be validated against history. The administrator is not interested in a theoretically intriguing model that cannot, at a minimum, predict the past well.

The second requirement was for detail: *geographic* detail, *substantive* detail, and *time* detail. On the geographic side, information is needed at the census tract level,[a] because that is the level at which facilities are located and services are provided.

Substantively, it became clear that information on total population, total housing units or total jobs was not good enough; nor was the information contained in a single-dimension breakdown of a total, such as the age distribution of people or the income distribution of households or the price breakdown for housing. The administrator needs to know "joint" properties. That is, he needs to know who is old *and* well-educated *and* foreign-born, because people behave differently with respect to his organization depending upon precisely who they are in joint terms. These distinctions, which will be important later, can best be grasped from a simple table for an imaginary census tract.

		Education		
		Less Than High School	*High School or More*	*Total*
	Young	80	120	200
Age	Middle Aged	200	260	460
	Old	180	160	340
	Total	460	540	1,000

[a]The U.S. Census Bureau [6] defines census tracts as: "small, relatively permanent areas into

The total population of 1,000 is broken down into two single-dimension distributions—age (200, 460, 340) and education (460, 540)—and a joint distribution represented by the numbers in the individual cells.

So far as time is concerned, the administrator needs to know all these things at least once every year. Intervals of five or ten years are too coarse for the normal administrative planning cycle.

The administrator's third overall requirement was that the output of whatever we did had to be couched in the language of the organization, not the language of the social scientist. Administrators are not, in general, interested in households or housing units or jobs. They care about deposits or classrooms or workers or millions of cubic feet.

A Phenomenological Approach

From this perspective, we looked at recent attempts at projecting the future of regions. Because of complexity and size they were usually based upon a computer model of some sort. The approach, in most cases, can be diagrammed as follows:

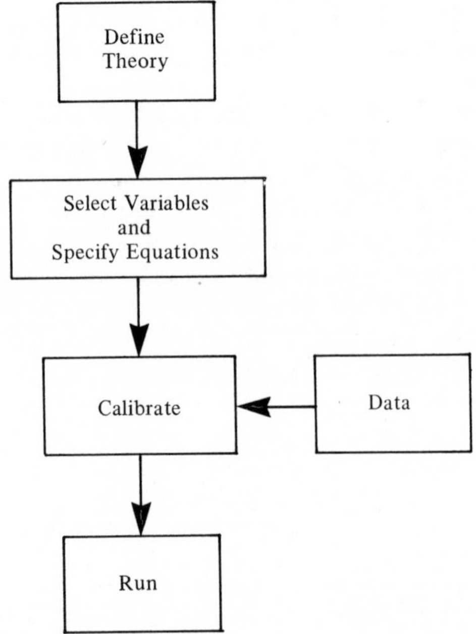

which large cities and adjacent areas are divided for the purpose of providing comparable small-area statistics. . . . Tracts are originally designed to be relatively homogeneous with respect to population characteristics, economic status, and living conditions; the average tract has about 4,000 residents.

This traditional approach starts with a set of theories. Once the theory is selected, the modeler specifies variables and the equations that relate them. The next step (called "calibration") is to obtain values for the coefficients in the equations using some statistical method such as regression analysis. The final step is to run the model and write a report. We call it a "grand design" approach because it starts at the beginning with a grand design of how the region works.

We were not very encouraged by what we found when we looked at the results to date of the grand design approach. In the first place, the theories were not very sound and were heavily contested in the literature. The specification and calibration stages were limited by traditional methods of analysis that rely primarily on the assumption that the best way to express the relationship of one variable to another is a straight line. The result was that most models built in this way did not do very well.

Regional modelers have developed several strategies to obscure this reality. One strategy, for example, is the "run into the future" strategy. The model is started at the present and runs into the future where no one can check its correctness. A variant on this theme is the "hypothetical city" strategy. The model describes a hypothetical city for which no one has data against which to make comparisons. A third strategy is the "problem focus" strategy. Using this strategy, the modeler models some specific problem, such as transportation or housing or pollution, and blames exogenous factors outside the model for the model's inadequacies. A fourth strategy is to make a simple model and apologize for its simplicity and/or impose exogeneous constraints to force it to come out right. None of these strategies is very satisfying, nor do they inspire great confidence on the part of a potential user. The outcome of most of these efforts has usually been a report, and little more.

We viewed most of these attempts at grand designs in much the same way Galileo is supposed to have viewed the scientists of his time who persisted in debating Aristotle's theory about the number of teeth in a horse's mouth. According to the story, which may be apocryphal, Galileo suggested that these scientists, instead of debating, might be better off finding some horses, opening their mouths, and counting. It was clear to us that many of the people fabricating grand designs were not, for the most part, counting teeth. A forthright statement by one of the more recent and empirically ambitious modeling efforts[b] sums it up well and begins to suggest some of the causes.

In the course of the research program, we stressed the use of sensitivity experiments as a means of identifying those parts of the model that are most sensitive and therefore most promising candidates for further research. The results of these sensitivity experiments depend, however, on the structure of the model, and the conclusions drawn from these experiments are therefore based on the assumption that the model structure is a valid representation of the real

---

[b]See Hamilton, et al [2].

world. The model's validity can be tested only by comparing its output to real world data. This may be done, for example, by seeing how well the model can reproduce past regional performance. Unfortunately, in attempting to conduct validation runs of this kind, our experience has been that obtaining reliable and comparable data for past years takes a great deal of effort and is extremely difficult. Although several runs of this type were made, because of these difficulties with the data, our original plans for conducting more extensive validation tests were abandoned.

The inference should not be drawn that no scholars have been immersing themselves in the realities of the phenomena causing urban change. The problem is that those closest to the phenomena have not been particularly quantitative or macroscopic in their analysis and that those of a quantitative bent have let their methodologies stand between them and reality. Perhaps the most obvious exception to this generalization is the attempt by Raymond Vernon and his colleagues to explain the changes taking place in the New York Metropolitan Region. In such publications as *Anatomy of a Metropolis,*[c] *Metropolis 1985,*[d] and *The Myth and Reality of Our Urban Problems*[e] we find a genuine effort to relate the observed quantitative shifts taking place in the region to the needs and aspirations of individuals and households and businessmen and landlords as they go about their day-to-day business.

The research described in this book began very much in that same spirit. We decided at an early stage that at the heart of any urban change lay the decisions of hundreds of thousands of individuals each year to get married, have children, buy a new house or rent a new apartment, relocate a business, lay a new foundation, or open up a new plant and that, if we were to understand how change took place, we had to understand these individual phenomena first. To make life somewhat easier, we picked New Haven rather than New York. We talked to hundreds of builders, real estate agents, businessmen, and college administrators about how they went about making decisions. We carefully studied surveys of individuals and households that purported to describe behavior. And we gathered any and all data we could find about what actually took place in New Haven, starting in 1638. As a matter of policy, we made few, if any, prior judgments about what we expected to find. Things had changed a great deal since *Anatomy of a Metropolis,* both in urban life styles and in the sources of data describing them. We avoided a commitment to any particular methodology or set of discipline-based theories on the assumption that they were overly restrictive and, in most cases, out-of-date. We stayed away from the computer for several years. In short, we mostly counted teeth.

---

[c]See Hoover and Vernon [3].

[d]See Vernon [4].

[e]See Vernon [5].

As the work progressed, one question was asked over and over again: How can we capture the essence of what we are observing in manageable form? Clearly, it was not possible, with present technology, to model the activities of every individual in New Haven every day. What gradually emerged in response to our question was the realization that, if we could group people according to the roles they were playing and the kinds of things they were doing in these roles, we could simplify the task of analysis without losing touch with the reality of day-to-day existence. Accordingly, we began to search for a set of roles for people and a set of "things they were doing"—which we called phenomena—that would be complete enough to explain the changes taking place and small enough to be manageable. The resulting list of roles, as it presently stands, includes:

Person (as a private individual).

Household Head.

Employer in the region.

Employer in another region.

Household head in another region.

Real Estate Agent.

Builder or Developer.

Planning Board Member.

Landlord.

Homeowner.

Mortgage Banker.

These are the kinds of people whose behavior we have found it useful to understand. The activities, or phenomena, in which we found them principally engaged include:

Households being formed.

Households migrating from region to region.

Households relocating in the region.

People getting more education.

Women bearing children.

People dying.

People getting older.

People searching for and finding employment.

Buildings being built.

Zoning ordinances being passed.

Real estate negotiations taking place.

New businesses being formed.

Businesses going out of existence.

Businesses migrating in and out of the region.

Businesses expanding at their present location.

Businesses contracting at their present location.

Businesses relocating within the region.

Changes in the national economy.

Changes in other regional economies.

Our major task, of course, was to explain the observed phenomena in terms of the needs and desires and abilities of people acting in their various capacities. What has emerged is a structure like the one diagramed in Figure 3-1. In this diagram, people acting in various capacities are indicated in circles, phenomena in boxes. As suggested in the key, an arrow from a person to a phenomenon implies that that person participates in the phenomenon. Households, for example, participate in the phenomenon of searching for a new neighborhood. An arrow going the other way suggests that a phenomenon influences the behavior of some person or persons. The activities of a zoning board, for instance, influence what a developer or builder in a community can and will do.

An individual, serving in different capacities, can be actively engaged in several different phenomena. During the day time, for example, a person might be self-employed as a builder. One evening a week he might serve on a town planning board and he might also be taking a course at a local community college, thereby extending his education. He is, throughout all these activites, head of a household and may at some time decide to move to a new house.

Each phenomenon, of course, potentially involves the actions of several different kinds of individuals. The typical real estate negotiation, for example, involves a buyer, a seller, a real estate agent, and a mortgage banker. Taken together, the phenomena shape most of the activities in the region. If enough of the important ones are present and if they are properly described and related to one another in terms of the behavior of people, they should be sufficient to explain and predict patterns of urban change.

The beauty of a structure of this sort is that it relates directly to what can be observed. The researcher can talk to a builder, determine how he goes about his business, and model his behavior as the builder himself describes it—rather than in terms of some more abstract economic concept.

The hazard of a direct, behavioral approach, of course, is that it requires an accurate understanding of how each type of urban person behaves under a variety of circumstances—the kind of knowledge that is not in great abundance. Our most fundamental decision was to try to acquire that knowledge, from the ground up when necessary, in order to employ a structure that could be based directly on observation.

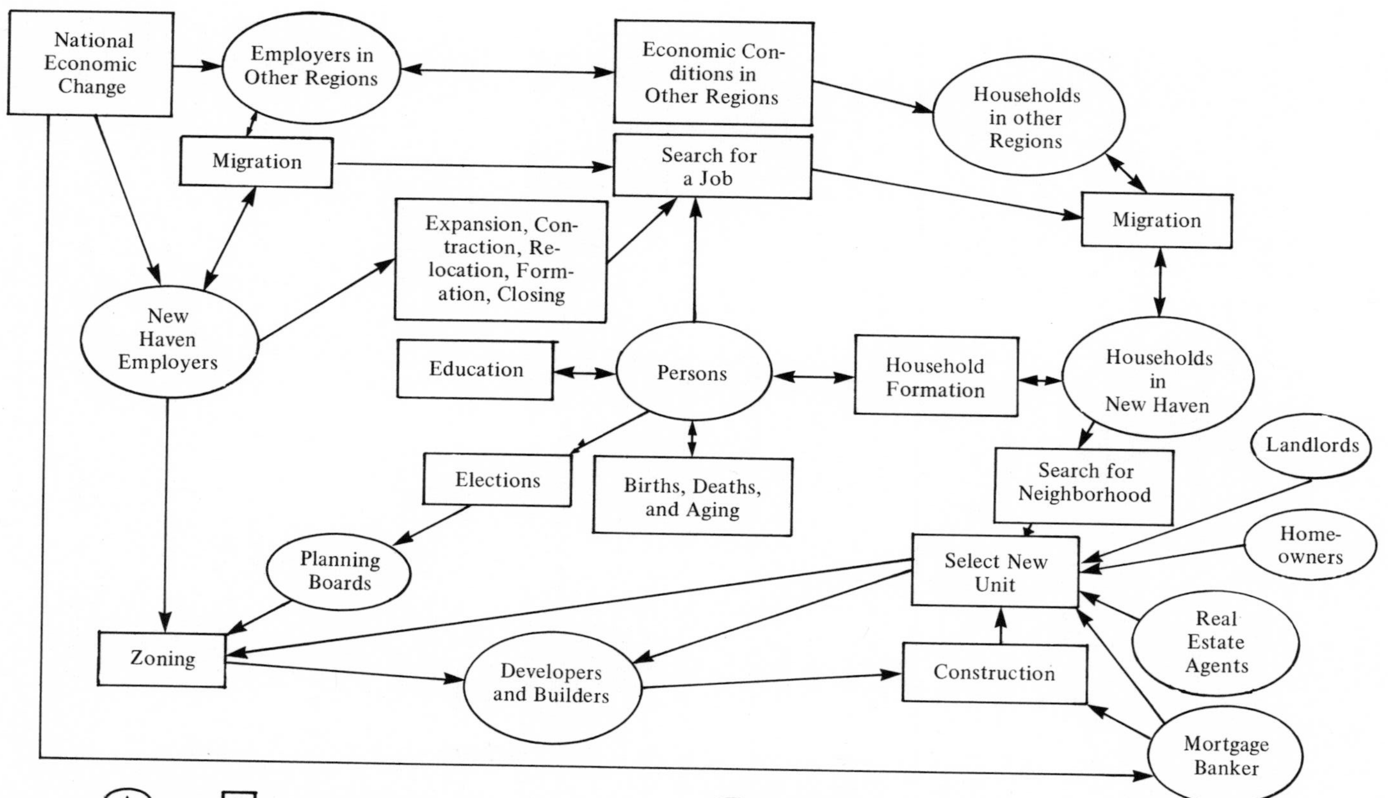

Figure 3-1 Phenomena and Actors in the New Haven Region

The Role of the Computer

As stated earlier, it is our view that the computer, like a cake pan in a bakery, belongs in the back room. The fact is, however, that we have made heavy use of computers, and in ways that might seem unusual to some. Whereas many others have used the computer to do faster that which they would have done previously by hand, we have used it to do things we would never have conceived of doing without it. In the process we have broken away from many of the traditional methods of analysis, and have made some primitive attempts to capitalize on the "free form" structure that the computer permits.

We have used the computer to do essentially three things: (1) reduce data, (2) reveal patterns in data, and (3) check the honesty of our theory. Over 200 computer programs[f] have been developed to perform these three functions. When they are all put together in one place, the resulting package is to the student of urban phenomena what the studio is to the artist or what the laboratory is to the physicist or chemist. It contains raw materials (data). It contains instruments for working with the raw materials and shaping them into theories. It contains a work bench on which the theories can be mounted and related to each other (a simulation model). And it contains monitoring devices for measuring the validity of the resulting product. It might be diagramed as in Figure 3-2.

We have called the approach being used by the "Person" in the center of the diagram an "iterative approach" because he or she goes through the loop (implied by the arrows on the diagram) iteratively thousands of times before the model "settles down" and the predictions can be relied upon with some confidence. During this iterative process, the theories are being constantly revised in response to their observed behavior in the model. The whole process is surrounded, as it were, by data.

When the model is becoming stable and predictions can be made confidently, attention focuses on translating the results into language that has meaning for the individual organizations that prompted our inquiry in the first place.

A Note on Accuracy

Implicit in the iterative approach is some notion of accuracy—the accuracy with which a model is replicating the "real world." We have chosen as our measure of accuracy simply the average percentage error between simulated results and actual data.[g] For any set of predictions about people or households or jobs,

[f]An introduction to these programs and how they fit together is provided in Appendix B. Appendix B in turn refers the reader to Birch, Atkinson, Sandström and Stack [1] for a still more detailed description.

[g]Other measures are possible, and modelers argue strenuously over which is best. For a brief

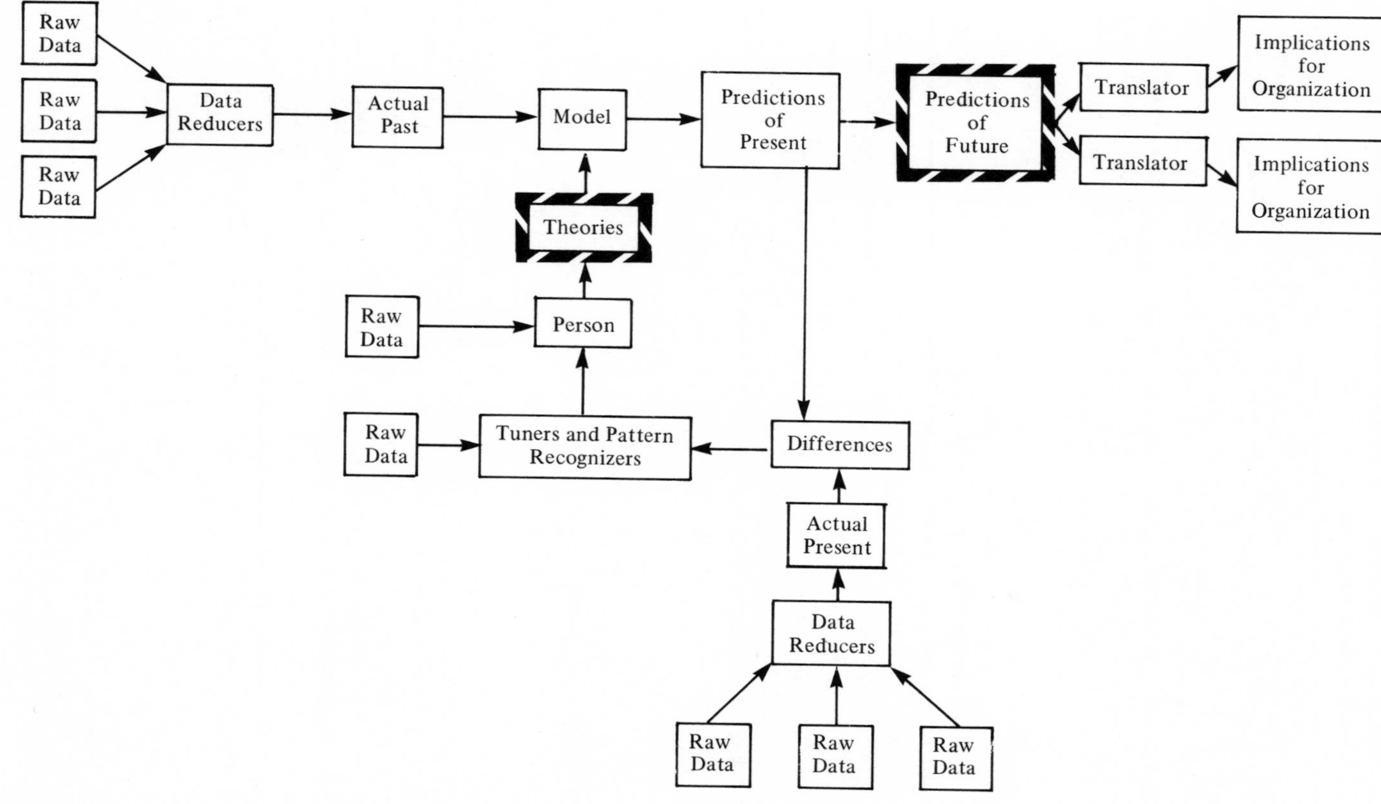

Figure 3-2 An Iterative Approach to Model Building

there are actually several different levels of substantive and geographic detail for which accuracy measures can be obtained. We can talk, for example, about the region as a whole, about towns or districts of the city within regions, and about the individual census tracts themselves. Similarly, for each level of geographic detail we can talk about total population (for example), or about marginal (or one-way) breakdowns.

To make matters slightly more complicated, none of the actual data is, in reality, "actual." No survey, from the Census on down, is completely accurate. Every "actual," is, in fact, an estimate. Furthermore, the greater the level of detail, the smaller the sample on which the estimate is based, and greater the uncertainty of the estimate.

From the modeler's point of view, there is little point in working further to reduce the average error when it is on the same order as the uncertainty of the "actuals" being compared against. Under these circumstances, there is no way of knowing whether the data or the model is wrong. It is necessary, therefore, to have some feeling for where this cutoff lies for each level of detail. Our estimates[h] of the percentage errors in the New Haven data for population and households are presented in Table 3-1.

We would expect, for example, that an estimate by the Census Bureau of the number of college educated people (a marginal) in Hamden (a district) might be off by ±5%. Throughout the remainder of this book we will refer to standards such as this in order to appraise the "robustness" of our theory.

Conclusions

When the simulation model shown in Figure 3-2 is running at approximately the measurement accuracy of the data, it has served its purpose. What remains of interest are: (1) the assumptions (or theories) about how the world works that emerged at the end of the iterative process, and (2) implications for the future.

What we shall do from this point on is "elevate" these two products of the laboratory for viewing and suppress the rest. We will go into some detail to describe the phenomena that appear to be generating change, and what happens when they interact with each other. We will also provide glimpses of what the future holds in store, if our understanding of the past and the present is correct, and try to give the reader some feeling for how critical our assumptions are.

---

discussion of this subject, the reader is referred to Birch, Atkinson, Sandström, and Stack [1], Section 10.

[h]These estimates were derived from error estimates published by the U.S. Census Bureau in their PHC (1) series. They have been adjusted upward when necessary to reflect the added uncertainty introduced by our own statistical operations on the data.

Table 3-1
Estimated Percentage Errors in New Haven Data for Population and Households

Level of Geographic Aggregation		Level of Substantive Aggregation: *Totals*	*Marginals*[1]	*Joints*
	SMSA	±1%	±2%	± 5%
	Town or District	±3%	±5%	±10%
	Tract	±5%	±9%	±20%

Source: Bureau of the Census [7]

[1]Henceforth, a single-dimension breakdown (that stands at the "margin" of a joint table) will be called a "marginal" distribution.

References

1. Birch, Atkinson, Sandström, and Stack. *The New Haven Laboratory.* Lexington, Mass.: Lexington Books, D.C. Heath & Co., 1974.

2. Hamilton, Goldstone, et.al. *Systems Simulation for Regional Analysis: An Application to River-Basin Planning.* Cambridge: The MIT Press, 1969.

3. Hoover, Edgar and Raymond Vernon. *Anatomy of a Metropolis.* Cambridge: Harvard University Press, 1959.

4. Vernon, Raymond. *Metropolis 1985.* Cambridge: Harvard University Press, 1960.

5. Vernon, Raymond. *The Myth and Reality of our Urban Problems.* Cambridge: Harvard University Press, 1962.

6. U.S. Department of Commerce. *1970 Census User's Guide: Part I.* October, 1970.

7. U.S. Bureau of the Census. *Census of Population and Housing: 1970, Census Tracts.* Final Report PHC(1)-142, Washington, D.C.: U.S. Government Printing Office, 1972.

4 Individuals and Households

The decisions of individuals and households to move to another neighborhood, to move to another region, to go to school, to have children, to vote, or to find a new job play a major role in shaping the growth of the region. Earlier we indicated in a general way some of the more significant shifts that have taken place as a result of individual decisions—the two major waves of migration from abroad that caused so much growth during the 19th century, the movement of households from the city into today's suburbs during the first half of the 20th century, the significant migration of minorities into New Haven since 1940 (introducing race as a major determinant of residential location), and the growing tendency of people of all kinds to look for a job as well as a house in the suburbs.

The patterns of change in the recent past can be seen in somewhat greater detail in Table 4-1. The minority population is singled out because of its influence during this period. Employment is also included to indicate the increasing independence of the suburbs. From the bottom line of Table 4-1 the reader can observe: (1) the relatively slow population growth of the region as a whole (less than one percent per year), (2) practically a doubling of the minority population, and (3) a rate of employment growth almost three times the rate of population increase.[a]

Upon careful inspection, it is clear also that almost all the growth has taken place in the suburbs. With the exception of Heights, Fairmont, Morris Cove, and Brookside-Rockview, central city neighborhoods are losing population. The city as a whole experienced a relatively modest (5 percent) growth in employment. The suburbs, in contrast, averaged a 27 percent increase in population and a 60 percent growth in employment.

As we move down to the neighborhood level,[b] the significance of race as a factor influencing residential location emerges more clearly. In neighborhood after neighborhood, minorities moved in in large numbers and whites moved out in even larger numbers. The overall effect of these shifts was a decline of 33,000

[a]Much of the imbalance between population and employment growth can be explained by the use of the 1960 SMSA boundaries in defining the region. Not included in the 1960 SMSA were the outlying towns of Bethany, North Branford, Madison, Milford, Wallingford, Ansonia and Derby. Many of these communities, while growing rapidly, are not yet self-sufficient in employment and "export" a labor force to the rest of the SMSA. In doing so, they absorb practically two-thirds of the total increase in employment.

[b]The 1960 census tracts contained in each of these neighborhoods are listed in Appendix A.

Table 4-1
Changes in New Haven Districts Between 1960 and 1970

Area	*Total Population*			*Minority Population*			*Employment*[1]		
	1960	*Change: 1960-70*		*1960*	*Percent Minority*		*1960*	*Change: 1960-70*	
Central City	*Pop.*	*Abs.*	*%*	*M. Pop.*	*1960*	*1970*	*Empl.*	*Abs.*	*%*
Brookside-Rockview	9,999	+ 294	+ 2.9	1,720	17.2	36.5	6,929	– 2,283	– 32.9
Westville	7,573	– 213	– 2.8	66	.9	4.0	154	+ 969	+629.2
Beaver Hills-Edgewood	15,513	– 2,273	–14.7	839	5.4	17.3	3,019	+ 1,119	+ 27.0
Newhallville	9,477	– 355	– 3.7	4,113	43.4	81.9	810	+ 1,104	+136.3
Dixwell	10,230	– 2,945	–28.8	7,580	74.1	85.2	3,902	– 893	– 22.9
Dwight	6,998	– 404	– 5.8	1,554	22.2	37.0	2,096	+ 1,661	+ 79.2
Hill	22,726	– 2,146	– 9.4	2,730	12.0	52.3	5,275	+ 445	+ 8.4
Central Bus. Dist.	1,292	– 616	–47.7	112	8.7	17.3	23,863	+ 7,842	+ 32.9
Whitney	15,551	– 800	– 5.1	924	5.9	15.9	10,727	– 1,251	– 11.7
Wooster Square	10,706	– 6,333	–59.2	2,648	24.7	37.0	10,231	– 3,316	– 32.4
Fair Haven	19,554	– 3,761	–19.2	1,000	5.1	18.5	8,792	– 1,399	– 15.9
Heights	5,672	+ 2,874	+50.7	59	1.0	13.6	935	+ 1,137	+121.6
Fairmont	4,628	+ 776	+16.8	29	.6	2.6	3,830	– 170	– 4.4
Morris Cove	4,789	+ 1,263	+26.4	2	.0	1.7	246	+ 475	+193.1
Longwharf	1,047	– 730	–69.7	265	25.3	4.4	7,317	– 852	– 11.6
Central City Total:	145,755	–15,369	–10.5	23,641	16.2	31.9	88,126	+ 4,587	+ 5.2

Suburbs									
Branford	16,609	+ 3,836	+23.1	169	1.0	1.9	3,582	+ 1,891	+ 52.8
East Haven	21,391	+ 3,771	+17.6	62	.3	.8	1,588	+ 1,594	+100.4
North Haven	15,936	+ 6,215	+39.0	236	1.5	3.1	9,573	+ 5,891	+ 61.5
Hamden	40,972	+ 7,547	+18.4	616	1.5	4.7	10,832	+ 4,385	+ 40.5
Woodbridge	5,181	+ 2,558	+49.4	65	1.3	1.9	399	+ 665	+166.7
Orange	8,544	+ 4,978	+58.3	29	.3	1.8	2,513	+ 2,272	+ 90.4
West Haven	42,479	+ 9,760	+23.0	873	2.1	6.2	8,478	+ 4,893	+ 57.7
Guilford	7,811	+ 4,225	+54.1	94	1.2	3.4	1,436	+ 1,412	+ 98.3
Suburban Total	158,923	+42,890	+27.0	2,144	1.3	3.8	38,401	+23,003	+ 59.9
Region Total	304,678	+27,521	+ 9.0	25,785	8.5	14.8	126,527	+27,590	+ 21.8

Source: Derived from U.S. Bureau of the Census [39, 34, 37, 32], Connecticut Labor Department [9, 10], New Haven Community Renewal Program [25].

[1] 1970 Employment figures are estimates made by our simulation model. They are based on a run to 1970 from 1967–the last point in time for which actual data was available.

in the non-minority central city population between 1960 and 1970. As we shall see shortly, most of the fleeing households took refuge in the surrounding suburban communities where they could find more attractive neighborhoods with better schools and vacant land on which to build more modern homes.

Four maps have been juxtaposed in Figure 4-1 to show the spatial distribution of these phenomena. The maps depict different levels of residential density, percent of households with income over $10,000, percent minority, and percent change in total population between 1960 and 1970. By mentally superimposing the maps, one can begin to see, in a slightly different way, the growth of the lower density, higher-class out-lying areas, the concentration of minority persons in the lower-class, more densely populated areas, and the overall decline in population of those areas that are experiencing influxes of minority persons. The movement of minorities into the suburbs was taking place at too low a level during the 1960's to be visible on this rough a scale, although it would show up in a similar set of maps for the 1970's, as will be seen shortly.

The Causes of Change

The patterns of change just described are still fairly coarse. Underlying these aggregates—and to a great extent giving them their shape—is the constant churning of individual decision-making. It is our basic premise that, to predict the aggregate accurately, the underlying dynamics of this individual decision-making must be understood; it is the only way to separate cause from correlation. We will proceed by first describing the underlying processes that seem to be causing change, and then observe how accurately a simulation based on our understanding of these processes reproduces aggregate effects that can be observed.

The discussion which follows is organized around four principal phenomena in which households and individuals are engaged: (1) natural increase; (2) shifts from type to type, (3) migration from region to region, and (4) local movement. Before going into detail, though, some rough feeling for the relative magnitudes of the different phenomena may be helpful.

In the region as a whole, all of the recent growth in population is attributable to natural increase (see Table 4-2). Between 1960 and 1970 the total increase of 27,521 consisted of an excess of births over deaths of 31,012 and a net out-migration of 3,491. In other words, most of the growth was generated from sources within the region and not outside it.

The situation was quite different for the individual towns. The city experienced a net out-migration of 30,000 people, compensated in part by natural increase of 15,000. The suburbs, in contrast, received almost two-thirds of their new inhabitants from other towns (movers) and from outside the region (migrants). Of the two, movers constituted about 70 percent of the total,

Table 4-2
Components of Population Change in New Haven, 1960 to 1970

Town	*Total Change*	*Natural Increase*	*Net Migration and Local Movement*	*Net Migration and Local Movement as a Percent of Total Change*
City of New Haven	−15,369	15,058	−30,427	−198.0%
Suburbs				
Branford	3,836	2,159	1,677	+ 43.7%
East Haven	3,771	2,686	1,085	+ 28.8
North Haven	6,215	1,591	4,624	+ 74.4
Hamden	7,547	2,415	5,132	+ 68.0
Woodbridge	2,558	344	2,214	+ 86.6
Orange	4,978	701	4,277	+ 85.9
West Haven	9,760	4,918	4,842	+ 49.6
Guilford	4,225	1,140	3,085	+ 73.0
Suburban Total	42,890	15,954	26,936	+ 62.8
Region	27,521	31,012	−3,491	− 12.7%

Source: Derived from Connecticut State Department of Health [11] and U.S. Bureau of the Census [39, 34].

outnumbering net migrants almost 2.5 to one. Local movement is clearly the dominant factor, much of it coming from the central city.

In our study of individuals and households, what emerges time and again is the fact that different kinds of individuals and households behave very differently, that it makes little sense to talk about "the" birth rate or "the" determinants of migration, and that the failure to disaggregate can lead to serious errors. An observer of the city of New Haven during the 1960's, might, for example, notice that "the" birth rate per 1,000 women declined only slightly during the decade, and assume that the substantial nationwide decline in family size did not apply in New Haven. What happened, of course, was that the mix changed; whites moved out and blacks moved in. While the birth rate for both groups is declining, the rate for blacks is still considerably higher; hence the slow decline in the composite. Frequently, we must know "who" and not just "how many."

The decision to disaggregate poses a difficult problem—what categories should be used? Too many categories means too large an analysis, too little data for each category, and a great deal of uncertainty. Too few categories, on the other hand, means making very gross assumptions; in the extreme case, it means treating all people as though they behaved in the same way regardless of age, education, ethnic background, income and so forth. The problem is further complicated by the fact that no single characteristic, by itself, seems to explain

Persons per
Square Mile
(1967)

....	Less than 4,000
++++	4,000 to 8,000
0000	8,000 to 16,000
@@@@	Over 16,000

Percent of Families with
Income Greater than $10,000
(1967)

....	Less than 30%
++++	30% to 50%
0000	50% to 65%
@@@@	Over 65%

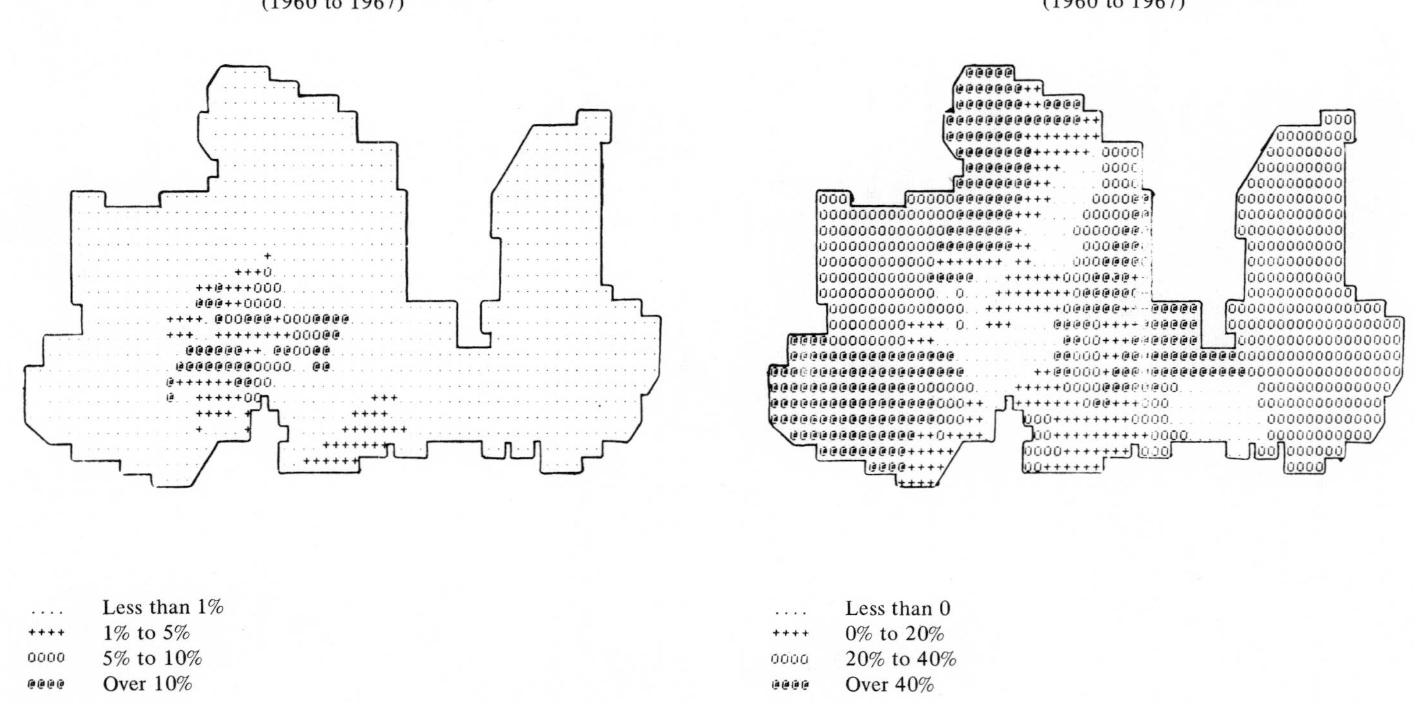

Figure 4-1 Measures of Income, Residential Density, Change in Percent Minority, and Percent Change in Total Population in New Haven's Residential Districts During the 1960's

behavior very well. Young people, for example, do not all behave the same way. Their behavior depends upon the fact that they are young *and* have a certain ethnic background. In other words, it is their *joint* properties that count, not any single property, or collection of single properties, such as age and income.

Under these circumstances, the key is to isolate those dimensions which "carry" the greatest amount of information. Age and education are a good set of dimensions because they describe quite different aspects of a potential migrant or homeowner. Age, educational attainment, and income are a poor set because income "takes up space" and adds very little new information. For any particular ethnic group in a selected age category, income and educational attainment are highly correlated; knowing one, the other is, for the most part, redundant.

After considerable investigation we observed that age and ethnic background were absolutely essential. Young people behave very differently from old people in response to different sets of needs. Similarly, the native, foreign-born, and minority populations in New Haven live in different kinds of neighborhoods, work at different kinds of jobs, and live in different kinds of housing units. A third essential dimension is social status. High-status people have different preferences (and abilities to pay for them) than low-status people, and this has a good deal to do with where they live, where they work, and so forth. Our inititial instinct was to use income as a measure of status. We found, however, that income was not a particularly good discriminator. An electrician and a lawyer, both earning $15,000 per year, behave very differently when they select housing units and neighborhoods and places of employment. A far more discriminating dimension is educational attainment. As so many parents who urge their children to stay in school have assumed, education has a big effect on what jobs a person holds, where he or she lives, how many children are born, and many other things. We finally settled, therefore, on age, ethnic/racial background, and educational attainment, broken down as follows, for our categories:

Dimension	*Categories*
Age	1. 0-19 2. 20-39 3. 40-64 4. 65-and over
Race/Ethnic[a]	1. Native (non-minority) 2. Foreign-born (non-minority) 3. Minority
Educational attainment	1. Less than 12 years 2. 12 years (High School) 3. Over 12 years

[a]The category "minority" includes blacks and Puerto Ricans. The "foreign-born" are all those who were born abroad *and* are not minority. Everyone else is "native."

We have found it useful to think in terms of the progression of each ethnic/educational combination through different age categories—the life cycle, if you will—that is, to arrange the 36 jointly defined types as shown in Table 4-3 (the numbers are people in the region in 1970):

Table 4-3
Population by Type of Person for the New Haven SMSA in 1970

		Native			*Foreign-Born*			*Minority*		
		<HS	*HS*	*>HS*	*<HS*	*HS*	*>HS*	*<HS*	*HS*	*>HS*
Age	0 - 19	84,787	4,134	968	1,330	53	32	22,780	774	130
	20 - 39	16,314	28,002	22,005	1,821	798	1,250	7,595	4,743	2,457
	40 - 64	33,335	23,775	21,062	6,346	1,899	1,333	6,510	1,360	939
	65 and Over	12,896	4,798	5,289	9,236	872	620	1,521	244	191

Source: Derived from U.S. Bureau of the Census [34, 37]

Households are defined along the same dimensions (by the characteristics of the household head), the only exception being that all household heads are assumed to be over 20 years of age. In reality, about two percent are less than 20 years of age. In our analysis they have been placed into the 20-39 category.

So much for rough magnitudes and definitions. Now it is time to look in some detail at the phenomena and the individual processes that are causing change. We will begin with natural increase.

Natural Increase

One of the advantages of working with New Haven is that, at least for the region as a whole, much of the growth is generated by two processes that are well understood and are regular—births and deaths. The death rates for each particular type of person (we shall call properties associated with individual household or population types "type-specific" henceforth) are quite stable over five and ten year intervals. The type-specific death rates (per 1,000 people) currently assumed for the New Haven region as of 1970 are presented in Table 4-4.

Aggregate birth rates (per 1,000 women) are changing, of course, but much of the change has been caused by a shift in the mixture of types of women (more of them are better educated and older), than in a shift in the type-specific rate itself. The type-specific rates for New Haven in 1970 are also shown in Table 4-4. Nothing unexpected is found in Table 4-4. Most of the births, of course, are

Table 4-4
Type-Specific Birth and Death Rates for New Haven in 1970

Births per 1,000 Women per Year

		Native			Foreign-Born			Minority		
		<HS	HS	>HS	<HS	HS	>HS	<HS	HS	>HS
Age	0 - 19	10	10	10	2	2	3	30	30	30
	20 - 39	150	150	130	100	100	100	180	170	140
	40 - 64	1	1	1	1	1	1	1	1	1
	65 and Over	0	0	0	0	0	0	0	0	0

Deaths per 1,000 People per Year

		Native			Foreign-Born			Minority		
		<HS	HS	>HS	<HS	HS	>HS	<HS	HS	>HS
Age	0 - 19	1	1	1	1	1	1	1	1	1
	20 - 39	2	2	2	3	3	3	4	4	4
	40 - 64	10	10	10	12	12	12	20	20	20
	65 and Over	55	64	45	75	79	89	97	61	25

Source: Derived from U.S. Bureau of the Census [35], Connecticut State Department of Health [11] and Bogue [4].

for women between the ages of 20 and 39. The higher rate for minority women and the lower rate for the foreign born (who are clustered at the "old" end of the 20-39 spectrum) are not unusual. It is worth noting, however, that with increasing education, the minority and nonminority birth rates approach each other. As more minorities enter college, the disparity in total births per 1,000 women should decrease.

Shift From Type-To-Type

Another set of phenomena that are largely internal to the region and that affect the mixture of people in it are those through which people and households change type—either through some inevitable process such as aging or becoming "native" (simply by virtue of being the child of foreign-born parents) or through changes in societal values and aspirations that lead to a deliberate change in status. Into this latter category fall the propensity to get a higher education, the propensity of individuals to form into households, and the propensity of people in general, and women and old people in particular, to join and remain in the labor force. While few, if any, of these propensities are static over time, when the type of person is taken into account, the changes are relatively slow and stable.

To see that these change-of-type phenomena have been actively at work in New Haven during the recent past,[c] one need only glance at the following shifts between 1960 and 1970:

Item	*1960*	*1970*
Percent People Foreign-Born	10.9%	7.7%
Percent Household Heads with College Education	22.1%	28.6%
Percent Household Heads with less than High School Education	56.9%	46.9%

By demographic standards, each of these shifts is significant over so short a time period, and each has contributed, in part, to the overall patterns of change in the region.

Of particular note is the increasing tendency of individuals to maintain separate households rather than living with relatives. This phenomenon is seen most easily in the type-specific headship rates—that is, the percent of each type of person that is a household head. The type-specific rates in 1970, and the percent change in each rate between 1960 and 1970, are presented in Table 4-5. As might be expected, the percent of persons acting as household head increases with age. Also, the trend toward more separate households holds true for all household types, particularly minorities. Apparently, the opening up of new neighborhoods to minorities (The Hill, Newhallville, Southern Hamden, and Fair Haven, for example) during the 1960's permitted many previously overcrowded minority families to "spread out" and form households of their own.

Migration From Region To Region

The migration of households into and out of the New Haven region is one of the more difficult phenomena to explain because much of the motivation for it lies outside the region. A household in Buffalo, for example, deciding where to move looks into job opportunities in several localities, talks to friends and makes a choice. Whether it chooses New Haven depends to a great extent upon how New Haven stacks up against all the others—information we do not have. In a more perfect world, we would have a model of all these decisions. Such a model would

[c]Some of these changes are due, of course, to changes in the mix of people moving into and out of the region. As we shall see shortly, however, the mix of in- and out-migrants is similar, and is not a likely cause of the shifts in the table.

Table 4-5
Type-Specific Headship Rates in 1970 and Changes Between 1960 and 1970 for New Haven

Type-Specific Headship Rates in 1970

		Native			Foreign-Born			Minority		
		<HS	*HS*	*>HS*	*<HS*	*HS*	*>HS*	*<HS*	*HS*	*>HS*
	20 - 39	.44	.31	.47	.29	.27	.53	.48	.36	.41
Age	40-64	.51	.45	.57	.55	.48	.72	.54	.36	.69
	65 and Over	.55	.58	.61	.55	.53	.66	.60	.56	.56

Percent Change in Type-Specific Headship Rates, 1960-1970

		Native			Foreign-Born			Minority		
		<HS	*HS*	*>HS*	*<HS*	*HS*	*>HS*	*<HS*	*HS*	*>HS*
	20-39	+6%	+4%	+ 7%	+2%	0%	−1%	+14%	+20%	+25%
Age	40-64	+5%	+4%	+ 9%	+3%	+4%	+6%	+15%	+22%	+26%
	65 and Over	+3%	+2%	+10%	+4%	+1%	+1%	+27%	+17%	+26%

Source: Derived from U.S. Bureau of the Census [39, 34, 37].

simulate the flow of jobs and households from each area to each other area each year. The flows into and out of New Haven would be a natural byproduct of the larger effort. Unfortunately, such a model does not exist, although bits and pieces of it can be found. The Census Bureau[d] and the National Planning Association[e] each make migration estimates for states and sometimes for SMSA's. Their procedures have been combined to produce a single estimate for each SMSA through 1980 by the MIT-Harvard Joint Center for Urban Studies as part of an attempt to estimate metropolitan housing needs.[f] In all cases, however, forecasts to date have been based upon extrapolation of past trends. Their saving grace is the stability of the trends.

We have attempted in our work to take advantage of systematic and nationally consistent forecasts where available and have supplemented them with internal adjustments to capture some of the year-by-year and type-by-type dynamics of the region. The analysis breaks into three parts: (1) an approxima-

---

[d]See U.S. Bureau of the Census [36].

[e]See National Planning Association [24].

[f]See Teplitz et.al. [31].

tion of the total gross in-migration and the gross out-migration in each year, (2) an estimate of the composition of that migration by household type, and (3) a prediction of the settling points within the region for in-migrants and the points of departure of out-migrants.

The level of gross, total annual in-migration and out-migration can be obtained from a combination of historical rates (as found in the Census Bureau's 509 by 509 migration tables[g] and the forecasts made by the Census Bureau and the National Planning Association and the Joint Center. All the estimates are very close—and hover around an average annual rate of three percent per year gross in-migration and three percent per year gross out-migration.

There remains the task of isolating the annual variations that are buried in the five- and ten-year average migration flows. The total in- and out-migration rates appear to vary with the relative performance of the New Haven economy vis-a-vis the national economy—as measured by unemployment rates. Thus, if the New Haven unemployment rate is lower than the national rate, in-migration picks up as people in other regions hear about the tight labor market and the resulting job opportunities in New Haven. Similarly, if the unemployment rate is higher than the national rate, the unemployed will tend to leave in search of other work, and the overall out-migration increases.

The tendency to leave when unemployment rates rise appears to be less than the tendency to in-migrate when the job market is tight. This must be in part a reflection of the attitude "if we wait long enough, things will get better" and the fact that out-migration appears to be less closely related to economic opportunities than in-migration. Old people out-migrate to the south, for example, upon retirement, not upon loss of job. Furthermore, both the tendency to stay and the tendency to in-migrate seem to depend upon the extent to which New Haven's unemployment rate varies from the national average—the greater the deviation, the greater the tendency to come or go.

These observations are based on an analysis of experience in the New Haven region between 1960 and 1970, when a great deal of fluctuation around the long-term averages took place. The region's economy is unusually dependent upon the munitions industry, since the city serves as a home for Olin, Winchester, Marlin, and Pratt and Whitney among others. The Vietnam buildup between 1963 and 1967 caused a rapid addition of 5,000 jobs in durable manufacturing—a sector that had been gradually declining over the previous ten years. Unemployment rates dropped to around 3 percent and workers flocked in. Between 1967 and 1970, the orders stopped, the jobs vanished, the unemployment rate rose to close to 9 percent, and many workers went elsewhere.

This set of events provides a classic example of dangers of basing any analysis and projection on data for only two points in time. If the experience between

[g]See U.S. Bureau of the Census [33].

1960 and 1967 were used for calibration purposes, the resulting employment curve for manufacturing might well look like that in Figure 4-2a, assuming a constant compound growth rate. The actual experience through 1972 is presented in Figure 4-2b. The differences in 1980 forecasts are substantial (55,000 jobs vs. 35,000), Figure 4-2b being by far the more realistic. More will be said on this point in the discussion of employment. It is in response to such unusual surges of employment in and out of the region that the adjustments to average gross migration flows must be made.

The surge of munitions jobs significantly affected the mix of migrants as well as the total number. In order to staff up quickly with experienced workers and managers, Olin and others had to bring in an older group of people that had worked in the industry in the past. In particular, they were older than the average in-migrant during recent history. This set of events is a specific example of a general phenomenon—namely, that the fluctuations of different sectors in the economy affect different types of households heads, and thus the composition of in- and out-migration. In this case, the buildup of munitions jobs caused an initial in-migration of about 5,000 middle-aged natives with a high school degree or less, many of whom moved out when the jobs dried up.

To capture effects such as these in a simulation model, we first determine a "normal" composition of in- and out-migrants, based on census data. The results are presented in Table 4-6. The large net in-migration of minority groups explains a good portion of the growth in minority groups during the 1960 to 1970 period in New Haven. Most migrants are, as is usually the case, young.

As indicated above, these normal, average mixes do not reflect year-to-year variations due to shifts in the economy. Thus far, however, the only adjustment we have found necessary is one to compensate for the unusually old age of those who responded to the Vietnam War buildup. The relative numbers of middle-aged natives must be increased for in- and out-migration as durable manufacturing jobs rise and fall respectively.

Once the number and composition of in- and out-migrants are known, the final step is to estimate where in-migrants are likely to settle and where out-migrants are likely to leave from. Once again, information for in-migrants is easier to obtain because of the way the Census Bureau reports its results. In New Haven, we have found that we introduce very little error by assuming that each household type settles into the same census tracts that movers of the same type within the region choose for themselves. The process by which that choice is made will be described shortly in some detail. For out-migrants, in the absence of any detailed data,[h] we have assumed that out-migrants of each type leave census tracts in proportion to the concentration of that type in each tract and the general turnover rate in that tract.

---

[h]More detailed data should be available from utilities in the area who maintain records for final billing purposes, and that source is currently being explored.

Table 4-6
Average Composition of Migrant Households for the New Haven SMSA, by Type of Household Head, 1960 to 1970

Percent Distribution of In-migrants

	Native			Foreign-Born			Minority		
	<HS	HS	>HS	<HS	HS	>HS	<HS	HS	>HS
Young	16.9%	17.4%	16.9%	0.3%	0.3%	0.4%	7.7%	2.8%	2.1%
Middle Aged	12.0%	4.4%	4.4%	0.6%	0.2%	0.2%	3.1%	0.3%	0.3%
Old	6.0%	1.0%	1.0%	0.7%	0.1%	0.2%	0.5%	0.1%	0.1%

Percent Distribution of Out-migrants

	Native			Foreign-Born			Minority		
	<HS	HS	>HS	<HS	HS	>HS	<HS	HS	>HS
Young	18.4%	19.0%	18.4%	0.7%	0.7%	0.6%	2.1%	0.8%	0.6%
Middle Aged	14.1%	5.1%	5.1%	1.2%	0.4%	0.4%	0.9%	0.1%	0.1%
Old	7.4%	1.2%	1.3%	0.7%	0.2%	0.1%	0.2%	0.1%	0.1%

Source: Derived from U.S. Bureau of the Census [33, 38].

Movement From Neighborhood To Neighborhood

Migration analysis deals, of course, strictly with households migrating into and out of the region. It says nothing about those households that move from housing unit to housing unit within the New Haven SMSA. As we suggested earlier, for New Haven, the movement of households from one place to another within the region is one of the most important phenomena causing change. Such movement led to much of the population decline of the central city and the expansion of the suburbs during the 1960's. As we shall see in subsequent chapters, it has a significant effect on the construction of housing and the location of employment opportunities as well.

Unfortunately, intra-regional movement is one of the least understood phenomena in the general field of regional analysis. Several partial theories have emerged;[i] few have been tested adequately at the census tract level. We thus had to develop much of our own theory. From our work to date, already it is

---

[i] See, for example, Hoover and Vernon [14], Hoyt [15], Pack [26, 27], Clarke [8], Smith [30], Butler [6, 7], Lansing [16], Birch [1], Morrison [20, 21, 22, 23], Lowry [19], Shryock [29], Rossi[28].

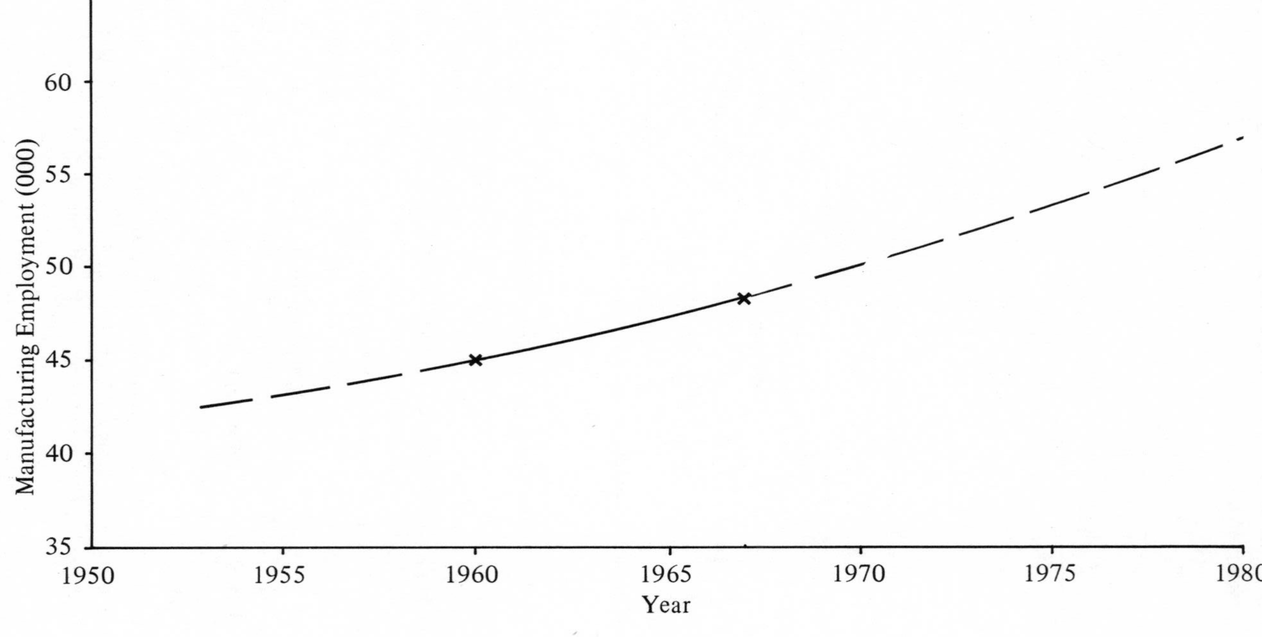

Figure 4-2a Two-Point Curve for Manufacturing Employment

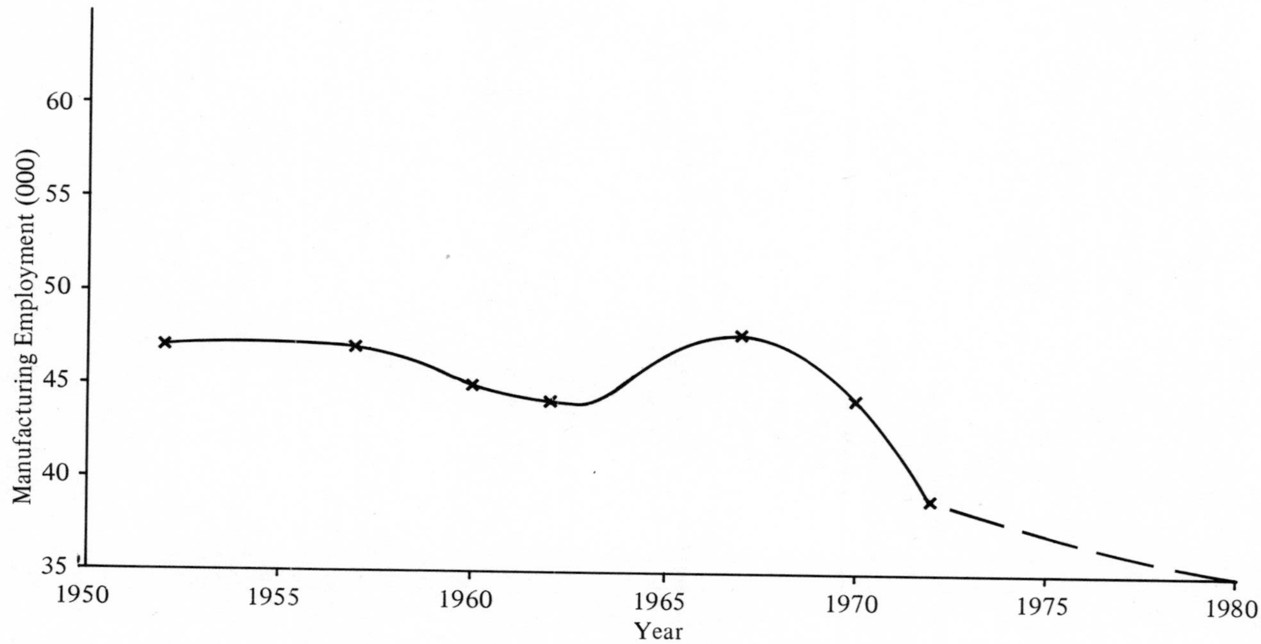

Figure 4-2b Multi-point Curve for Manufacturing Employment

clear that much of the conventional wisdom—or at least the wisdom incorporated into existing models—does not hold up very well.

We discovered first, as have others,[j] that we had to distinguish between "movers" and "stayers," i.e., those who choose not to move in any particular year. Movers tend to have distinctly different characteristics than people who stay put. They are younger, for one, and they tend to come from and move into apartments rather than single-family units. We assume initially that all households of a given type have the same chances of moving, regardless of what neighborhood they live in, and then modify this assumption as the realities of the tracts become known in greater detail.[k] Particularly important in this regard are changes in racial composition. As minorities move into a neighborhood, native and foreign-born households will increase their propensity to move until a new balance is established in the neighborhood.

Once the movers in each census tract, by type of mover, have been identified, there remains the task of understanding how they select a new housing unit in a new neighborhood. This decision appears to be a hierarchical one; that is, households first select a neighborhood, and then a housing unit within that neighborhood. The two decisions are related, of course. Households are not likely to look in neighborhoods that do not contain at least some suitable housing. But the suitability of the neighborhood dominates at the first pass. Richard Coleman[l] has observed the same hierarchical process in his interviews in Boston and Kansas City. As he puts it:

> When Americans living in metropolitan areas buy or rent a place to live, whether they be working class, middle class, or upper status, they tend first to determine which neighborhoods they will consider, and then settle on the house as a second decision.

Our model makes this same distinction. Each household type first selects those neighborhoods which it finds acceptable, and then begins its search for a unit. This chapter will focus on the first step of that two-step process—namely, the initial selection of a few acceptable neighborhoods. The next chapter will pick up on the selection of a unit within those neighborhoods, taking account of the details of housing availability.

At the heart of a behavioral theory of neighborhood choice is the calculus used by each type of household in deciding which neighborhoods to drive through on Sunday afternoons, and, ultimately, where to begin negotiating with homeowners or landlords over the price of a new unit. We started with a

---

[j]See particularly Butler [6].

[k]The initial estimates of the movement probabilities cannot be obtained directly from published sources, and must be derived from several sources. The procedure for deriving them is described in Birch, Atkinson, Sandström and Stack [3], Section 5, Appendix A.

[l]See Birch et.al. [2].

simple-minded "attractiveness score" concept to replicate the choice process. That is, we assumed that people considered several characteristics of a neighborhood (such as its "closeness," its density, its racial composition, its distance to work, and so forth), computed a "score" for each neighborhood based on a weighted average of the characteristics, and assumed that the higher the score, the greater the chances that people would move in.

Unfortunately, the attractiveness score approach did not work very well at the detailed tract-by-tract and type-by-type level. As we looked at the patterns in the errors we gradually began to realize a number of things. First, and most important, households about to move do not choose a new neighborhood by looking at all possible neighborhoods on a comparative basis. Rather, they eliminate all but a very few, almost subconsciously, and focus all their attention on the three or four that remain. In a region like New Haven, for example, young, college-educated native household heads might look in Guilford, sections of Hamden, and perhaps North Haven or Orange, depending upon their familiarity with the region, and eliminate all the rest without giving it much thought. They would, in all likelihood, avoid central city neighborhoods because of the turmoil in the schools, and would avoid most of the lower-class suburban neighborhoods simply out of a desire to "be with people like ourselves who like the things we like." A similar kind of pattern is followed by each other type, although the outcome in each case is, of course, potentially quite different.

One consequence of the initial filtering is the "cluster effect;" that is, people tend quickly to eliminate all neighborhoods that do not contain a substantial number of people like themselves. As Everett Lee[m] has observed for inter-regional migrants, the process of selecting a new area is done largely by word-of-mouth, and it is not surprising that people, in the process of talking with one another, tend to learn about a relatively few neighborhoods where similar people are located. Each New Haven neighborhood has, after all, evolved gradually over hundreds of years. Each has developed a reputation and a status and a "clientel" that is known to most other people in New Haven, or at least to those in the immediate vicinity. If one is forced to make a best guess, therefore, about where any particular type of person is likely to look for a house, it is in neighborhoods where people like themselves are already located in large numbers.

The clustering phenomenon, left strictly to its own devices, would lead to a collection of stable, homogeneous neighborhoods that change barely at all over time. What we observe (see for example Table 4-1) is quite different. Neighborhoods do change. "New" people move in and "old" people move out in search of something better. What must be explained, therefore, is not only the strength of the clustering effect, but the forces acting at the margin that continually undermine it and, in the process, change the locations where

[m]See Lee [18].

different types of people end up living. After much experimenting, we have found that a relatively few factors explain most of the change in existing neighborhoods. They fall into three categories–minority concentration, social status, and age of neighborhood.

Minority concentrations affect different people in different ways. Some people are sensitive simply to the concentration of minorities–the percent of the total that minorities constitute. Others care about the rate at which the percent is changing. That is, they are sensitive to whether the neighborhood is experiencing a significant increase in the percent minority. Still others care about both things at the same time. They want to know the present level *and* the rate at which it is changing.

Needless to say, minorities and non-minorities view these levels and changes quite differently. Minorities tend to move quickly into any neighborhood that is "opening up," from their perspective–that is, any neighborhood whose level is above some cutoff, such as 5 percent or 10 percent, and whose rate of minority increase is significant. Native and foreign-born households, in contrast, will tend to avoid such neighborhoods and will move out of them when the change begins to take place. In combination, those two sets of behavior lead to the so-called "tipping" phenomenon observed in so many urban areas in the United States.

Social status has to do with the "classiness" of a neighborhood as perceived by households in the region. There appears to be a well-defined pecking order, with Woodbridge and sections of Hamden at the top and Dixwell and sections of The Hill and Wooster Square at the bottom. For analytical purposes, we have tried to capture this pecking order by defining a neighborhood scale[n] from 1 to 5 where:

5 = Elite
4 = Upper Middle Class
3 = Middle Class
2 = Working
1 = Poor

The "classiness" of each neighborhood is derived from four of its characteristics:

1. Average Family Income
2. Average Educational Attainment
3. Land Use (percent land in industrial and commercial uses)
4. Occupation (professional and managerial are "high"; service workers are "low").

---

[n]Coleman [2] has defined a similar scale (based more on the type of housing in the neighborhood) that contains the categories: Very Good and Prestige Class Housing, Pleasantly Good, Standard Comfortable, Standard Marginal, and Substandard/Slum.

We find that, in almost all cases, the four dimensions are highly correlated; a neighborhood that is Upper Middle on the income dimension is very likely to be Upper Middle also on occupation, land use, and educational attainment. The dimensions are thus somewhat redundant. Household types that are upwardly mobile—particularly young and middle-aged ones—will tend to avoid the lower end of the status scale and select from among the top of the list of neighborhoods that are within their reach, regardless of whether or not people like themselves have done so in the past.

A related phenomenon is associated with the "age" of a neighborhood.[o] Some people prefer the new to the old. They want to live in a new unit with new and modern appliances in a new neighborhood that does not have all the problems of the old one they are now living in. They will sacrifice somewhat their relationships with friends and family of the same type in order to acquire more pleasing physical surroundings. With a little luck, they can have both if they can persuade others like themselves to join them.

Most notable by its absence from this list of factors that undermine the cluster effect is access to place of work and, by implication, the effect of the relocation of jobs upon where people live. We started out with the assumption that access to work had a big effect and gradually, in the face of empirical reality, came to the conclusion that it has been over emphasized as a determinant of urban structure—at least for changes in the recent past.

Survey results show that people's attitudes towards traveling to work do not reflect so much an interest in convenience as an interest in avoiding inconvenience. That is, people seem to have a tolerance (that averages remarkably close to 35 minutes for most people in most cities) below which travel time does not matter much, and above which it matters a great deal. The nature of the relationship between access time from a neighborhood to the household head's place of work and odds of selecting that neighborhood as a residential location is much more like the one in Figure 4-3b than the one in Figure 4-3a. Most important for our purposes is the fact that the curve in Figure 4-3b does not begin to "fall off" until a threshold of about 35 minutes driving time—out beyond New Haven region boundaries under most circumstances. In a special survey of movers conducted by Janet Pack [p] in New Haven in 1967, for example, access time to jobs was ranked 13th on a list of 25 factors considered in the choice of residential location, and change of job was ranked 18th. Similar

---

[o]Since we do not keep detailed track of the age of the housing stock in our model we have used as a surrogate the level of building activity in the neighborhood. "New" neighborhoods are ones in which a good deal of development is taking place. As the neighborhood "ages," the level of construction and population growth decrease, and eventually turn negative (abandonment). The average "age" of the neighborhood is assumed to increase during this life-cycle process.

[p]See Pack [27].

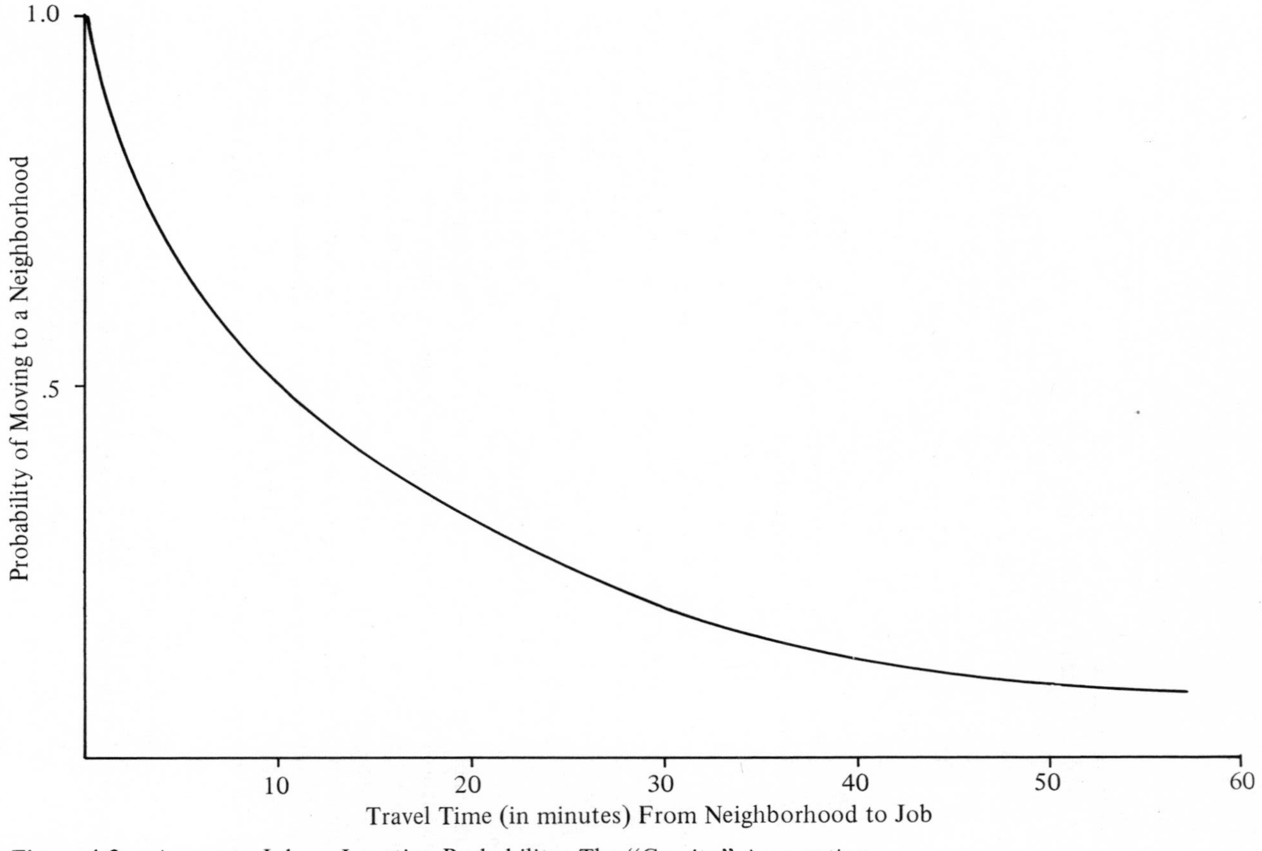

Figure 4-3a Access to Job vs. Location Probability: The "Gravity" Assumption

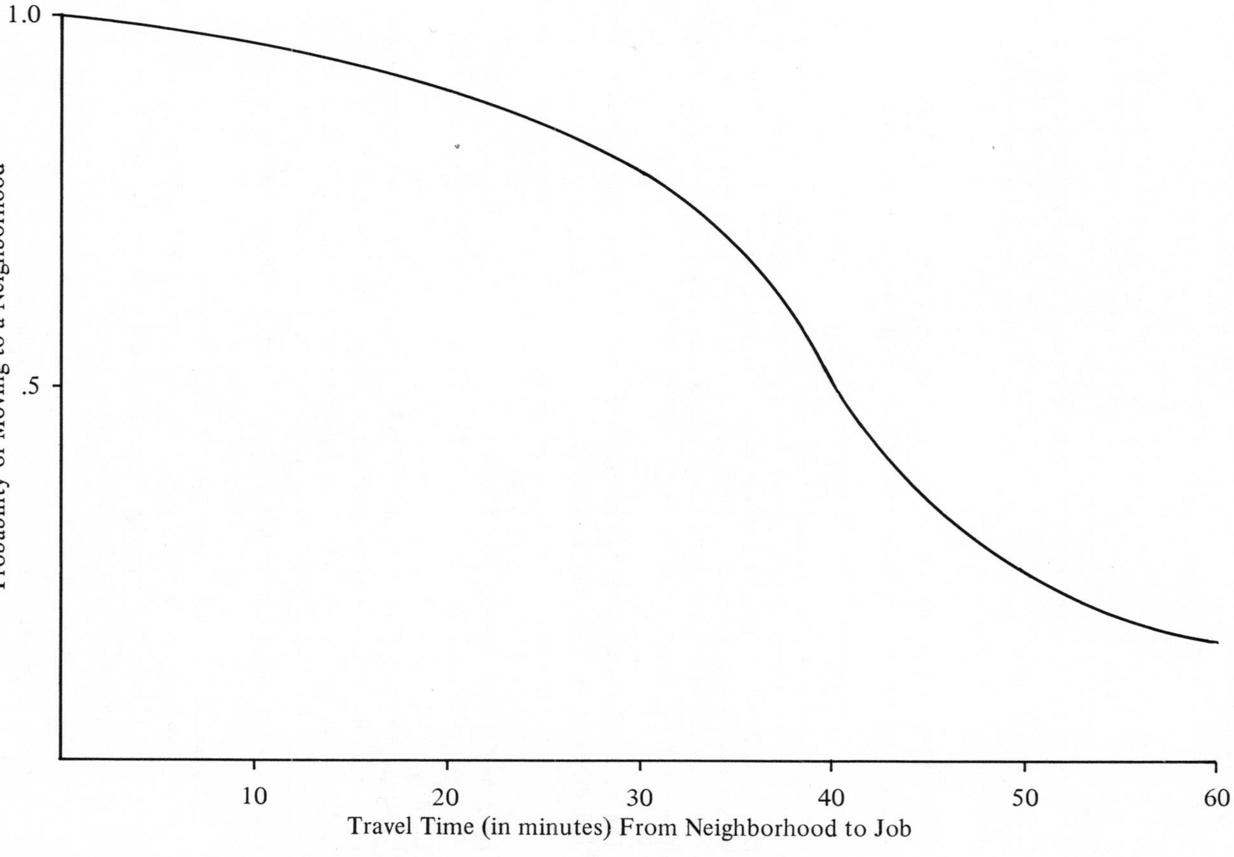

Figure 4-3b Access to Job vs. Location Probability: A "Threshold" Assumption

surveys by Butler et. al, Lansing and Hinshaw and Allott have revealed much the same thing.[q]

This realization has not come easily to urban modelers. Douglass Lee,[r] in his article "Requiem for Large-Scale Models" observes:

> Trip distribution functions (the heart of any gravity model, which includes most of the land-use models) are fitted to observed trip frequencies for different classes of workers and (sometimes) different classes of households. While valid at the scale of a metropolitan area, the gravity model has no statistical explanatory power at the neighborhood level. This is a near-classic case of imputing individual (or census tract or neighborhood) behavior from aggregate relationships—the ecological fallacy.

Yet modelers persist, and one cannot help being reminded by their persistence of the celebrated letter from Galileo to Kepler,[s] which reads, in part:

> Oh, my dear Kepler, how I wish that we could have one hearty laugh together. Here at Padua is the principal professor of philosophy, whom I have repeatedly and urgently requested to look at the moon and planets through my glass, which he pertinaciously refuses to do. Why are you not here? What shouts of laughter we should have at this glorious folly. And to hear the professor of philosophy at Pisa labouring before the grand Duke with logical arguments, as if with magical incantations, to charm the new planets out of the sky.

The notion that each additional minute of travel time significantly reduces the desirability of a neighborhood dies hard.

How the Choice is Made

Identifying the factors that do seem to alter the clustering tendency solves only half our problem. There remains the task of understanding how these factors enter into the decision-making processes of households deciding where to move. We have found that the way in which households employ different kinds of factors is quite type-specific. There is no universal set of factors or filters that everyone uses. Some households exclude all neighborhoods that are above or below some acceptable limit. Minority households, for example, tend to avoid neighborhoods with very high (greater than 75 percent) minority concentrations—for reasons we will explain shortly. Native and foreign-born households avoid any substantial minority concentrations. College-educated household heads avoid low status neighborhoods, and so forth.

---

[q]See Butler et. al. [6], Lansing [16], Hinshaw and Allot [13].

[r]See Lee [17].

[s]See Burtt [5].

Other households consider several neighborhood characteristics in combination when reaching a decision where to move. Native, college-educated households, for example, tend to avoid neighborhoods that are high class *and* very old in favor of the newer high-class communities. Older minority households are prone to avoid neighborhoods with relatively low concentrations (10 percent to 20 percent) of other minority households *and* a relatively low rate of minority increase (3 percent to 10 percent over a ten-year period). They apparently prefer to leave the entering of these hard-to-penetrate areas to the younger generation. In each case, it is a combination of properties that counts; no single property alone is sufficient to isolate the undesired neighborhood.

Although each individual household type uses at most three or four such screens or filters to alter its existing pattern of location, as indicated above, the choice of filters varies a great deal from type to type. We define a fairly large number of possible filters based on cutoffs for the individual characteristics—minority concentration, change in minority concentration, social status, and age—and also several possible combinations of minority conposition and minority change and of social status and age, since these two pairs of characteristics seemed to explain a great deal of the deviation from the tendency to cluster. We use the computer to determine which two or three filters are most appropriate for each household type.[t]

The final result is not easily presented in tabular or graphical form since it involves the selection among 118 filters by 27 different household types. What we shall do instead is describe some of the dominant patterns, of which some examples have been given above, and refer the specialist elsewhere for the detailed tables. The household types that appear to be deviating most from their traditional settling places fall into four main groups: (1) middle-class natives, (2) college-educated natives, (3) minorities, and (4) old and foreign-born (who are mostly old) households.

Middle-class natives are feeling the pinch of minority settlement more than most. For years they found a comfortable existence in the "industrial-revolution housing" in the central city. The influx of minorities has apparently been intolerable for them, and they have been abandoning their traditional neighborhoods for suburban housing wherever they could find it. Since the suburban housing market has always been tight, this "bailing out" of the middle class has led to the construction of a large number of new units—an increasing percentage of them apartments and town houses as the costs of land and labor and building materials make single-family units for the middle class less and less feasible. These middle-class households are trying desperately to avoid the lower class neighborhoods in the suburbs and the associated threat of another move before too long.

Minority households are experiencing the opposite side of the same coin.

---

[t]The procedure by which this is done is described in Birch, Atkinson, Sandström and Stack [3], Sections IV and V.

They are constantly searching for neighborhoods where the percent minority is above some threshold (usually around 3 percent to 5 percent) and the projected ten-year increase in this percentage is large. As the number of minority households has increased, this constant pressure on "weak spots" such as Newhallville and Fair Haven, has led to the "tipping" of block after block in several areas in New Haven and in a few neighborhoods across the city boundaries in West Haven and Hamden. As indicated above, minority households have no more interest in predominantly minority neighborhoods than native households do and would much prefer the more "newly entered" communities where they expect (and frequently find) better schools, better housing units, better recreational facilities, and so forth. Despite their success in breaking into several neighborhoods in the region during the 1960's, minorities are still not entering some areas that have, in one way or another, managed to exclude them. Morris Cove, East Haven, Orange and Woodbridge are good examples.

The college-educated natives in New Haven exhibit a mixed pattern. Unlike their less well-educated counterparts, they do not go out of their way to avoid minorities so long as the concentrations are "reasonable." They appear, as it were, to be experimenting with multi-racial living. At the same time, they prefer new, high-class suburban areas that have low minority concentrations like Orange and Guilford and Northern Hamden. It is difficult to sort out how much of an affect Yale is having on this pattern. Undoubtedly some of the experimenting is being done by Yale graduate students and faculty as they strive for ways to stay close to the University with its central location and its liberal tradition. We cannot, however, totally discount the young professionals, who have experienced multi-racial education at the college level on a large scale in recent years and who have made the adjustment more easily than some of their older and less well-educated colleagues. Whatever the cause, race is not the deterrent at the top of the social hierarchy that it is elsewhere—at least for some.

The older, non-minority households—a category that includes most of the foreign born ones—do not move very often. But when they do, they do their best to avoid declining, lower class neighborhoods, particularly those into which minorities are moving. The older minority households (which number very few) are equally eager to avoid the declining areas and the areas with large minority concentrations.

Summarizing, a household searching for a new place to live within the region seems to be torn between two kinds of desires. One is its desire to live near households of the same type; the other is its desire to upgrade its living environment. As neighborhoods change—particularly with respect to racial composition, social status, and age—the desire to upgrade is constantly undermining the tendency to cluster. As a result, "old" households are constantly moving out and "new" ones are constantly moving in. There is no concept of equilibrium. The entire history of New Haven's neighborhoods is one of transition, not of steady-state, and the recent past has been no exception.

Predictive Accuracy

The question naturally arises at this point: How well can all these assumptions about how people behave (when placed in a simulation model) describe how the world has actually worked over the past decade. In an iterative approach such as ours, it is a question that has been asked and answered thousands of times. For some initial sets of assumptions, out of which the ones described above have grown, the answer was: "Not very well." As our knowledge has increased, the answer has been "better and better." For the set just described, the answer is "not too badly."

The answer depends, of course, on what one means by "well." As indicated in Chapter 3, we have chosen as our measure simply the average error between simulated results and actual data. When we say "not too badly" about a simulation result, what we mean is that the average errors between the model and the actual data are on the same order as the measurement accuracy of the data used. Table 4-7 presents the actual errors between simulated results and actual data for households and population at various levels of substantive and geographic detail. The table also includes the estimated accuracy of the data being compared against—the target, if you will. As can be seen from the table,

Table 4-7
Average Percent Error for Population and Households in 1967 for 1960-1967 Run and Estimated Accuracy of the Data

		Simulated vs. Actual		
		Totals	*Marginals*	*Joints*
Population	SMSA	.6%	1.5%	4.9%
	District	4.1%	7.8%	14.3%
	Tract	6.9%	11.2%	19.6%
		Totals	*Marginals*	*Joints*
Households	SMSA	.2%	1.4%	2.9%
	District	2.2%	7.0%	15.0%
	Tract	3.9%	10.2%	21.2%
		Uncertainty in "Actuals"		
		Totals	*Marginals*	*Joints*
	SMSA	±1%	±2%	± 5%
	District	±3%	±5%	±10%
	Tract	±5%	±9%	±20%

the computer model based on our behavioral assumptions is simulating at, or close to, the measurement accuracy of the data in most cases. This particular table reflects the results of a run from 1960 to 1967, an intermediate point for which data are available due to a 1967 pretest of the 1970 census. The availability of this pretest, and hence the availability of three points instead of two, was a major reason for selecting New Haven as a study region. The same level of accuracy is obtained in runs from 1967 to 1970. Obvious exceptions lie beneath these averages, of course, and it is these exceptions that continue to stimulate the improvement of the theory.

Summary and Conclusions

In this chapter we have followed a pattern that we will follow in the next two. We began by outlining some of the basic changes that have taken place in the region. We then ask: What assumptions must be made about the behavior of people and households in order to explain the changes that seem to be taking place? A description of the assumptions is followed by a brief discussion of the accuracy with which a simulation model based on the assumptions has been able to replicate the past–neighborhood-by-neighborhood and type-by-type. No effort has been made to describe the mechanics of the simulation–just the essence on which it is based. The technically inclined reader is referred elsewhere for details.

Stepping back for a minute, one can see that the assumptions we have been forced to make (after thousands of "cut and fit" iterations) about how people grow up, form into households, and select a place of residence give us our first detailed indication that the basis for future growth in New Haven will be different from what it has been in the past. The earlier dependence on transportation and access to work no longer dominates. With relatively easy access for most people to any place in the region (either by car or by bus), attention shifts toward more sociological and aesthetic considerations–the problems of race, social status, the "newness" of neighborhoods, and so forth. Households are forming at an increasing rate, and about 1,000 more of them are leaving the central city each year than are moving into it. Most of them are heading out to the suburbs, and many are working in jobs that they are finding there.

We must suspend judgement on the exact nature of this process, however, until the other phenomena governing change–and their relationship to one another–are better understood.

References

1. Birch, D.L. "Toward a Stage Theory of Urban Growth," *Journal of the American Institute of Planners.* May, 1971.

2. Birch, Atkinson, Clay, Coleman, Frieden, Friedlander, Rainwater, and Teplitz. *Toward Housing Goals for the United States: Concepts, Methods, and Measures.* MIT-Harvard Joint Center for Urban Studies, August, 1973.

3. Birch, Atkinson, Sandström and Stack. *The New Haven Laboratory.* Lexington, Mass.: Lexington Books, D.C. Heath & Co., 1974.

4. Bogue, Donald J. *Principles of Demography.* New York: John Wiley and Sons, 1969.

5. Burtt, Edwin A. *The Metaphysical Foundations of Modern Science.* Garden City: Doubleday and Company, 1955.

6. Butler, E.W. and F.S. Chapin et al. *Moving Behavior and Residential Choice: A National Survey.* Highway Research Board, 1969.

7. Butler, E.W. and E. Kaiser. "Prediction of Residential Movement and Spatial Allocation," *Urban Affairs Quarterly.* June, 1971.

8. Clarke, W.L. *Intra-Metropolitan Migration and Town Characteristics.* Unpublished thesis, Massachusetts Institute of Technology, 1967.

9. Connecticut Labor Department. *Department of Connecticut Manufacturing and Mechanical Establishments.* Hartford, Connecticut: State of Connecticut, 1960 and 1967.

10. Connecticut Labor Department. *Employment by SIC Code in the New Haven Labor Market Area.* Unpublished Tabulations, Hartford, Connecticut, Various Years.

11. Connecticut State Department of Health. *Registration Reports: 1960 to 1970.* Hartford, Connecticut: State of Connecticut, 1963 to 1972.

12. Greater New Haven Chamber of Commerce. *Economic Profile and Industrial Directory: 1973-1974.* New Haven, Conn.: Greater New Haven Chamber of Commerce, 1973.

13. Hinshaw, Mark and Kathryn Allott. "Environmental Preferences of Future Housing Consumers," *Journal of the American Institute of Planners.* March, 1972.

14. Hoover, E.M. and R. Vernon. *Anatomy of a Metropolis, Part III.* Cambridge, Mass.: Harvard University Press, 1959.

15. Hoyt, H. *The Structure and Growth of Residential Neighborhoods.* Washington, D.C.: Federal Housing Administration, 1939.

16. Lansing, John B. *Residential Location and Urban Mobility: The Second Wave of Interviews.* Survey Research Center, University of Michigan, 1966.

17. Lee, Douglass B. "Requiem for Large-Scale Models," *Journal of the American Institute of Planners.* May, 1973.

18. Lee, Everett. "A Theory of Migration," *Demography* (1966), pp. 47-57.

19. Lowry, I.S. *Migration and Metropolitan Growth: Two Analytical Models* Chandler, 1966.

20. Morrison, Peter. *Alternate Models of Population Mobility.* Proceedings of Cornell Conference on Human Mobility, 1968.

21. Morrison, Peter. *Population Movements and the Shape of Urban Growth: Implications for Public Policy* (Prepared for the Commission on Population Growth and the American Future) 1972.

22. Morrison, Peter. *The Propensity to Move: A Longitudinal Analysis* Prepared for the U.S. Department of H.U.D., 1971.

23. Morrison, Peter. *Theoretical Issues in the Design of Population Mobility Models.* The RAND Corporation, 1969.

24. National Planning Association. *Regional Demographic Projections, 1960-1985,* Report No. 72-R-1, Regional Economic Projection Series. Washington, D.C., 1972.

25. New Haven Community Renewal Program. *Connecticut-Industrial Floor Area Block Summary and Average Rating.* Technical Paper No. 8, New Haven, Connecticut, 1964.

26. Pack, Janet. *CDAP Demographic Study.* New Haven City Planning Department, 1969.

27. Pack, Janet. *Movers Survey: Some Dimensions of the Housing Market in the City of New Haven.* New Haven City Planning Department, 1969.

28. Rossi, P.H. *Why Families Move.* Glenco: Free Press, 1955.

29. Shryock, H.S. and J.S. Siegel. *Methods and Materials of Demography,* Chapter 21. U.S. Census Bureau, Washington, D.C.: Government Printing Office, 1971.

30. Smith, W.E. "Forecasting Neighborhood Change," *Land Economics.* August, 1963.

31. Teplitz, P., D.L. Birch and B. Frieden. *Forecasting Metropolitan Housing Needs.* Joint Center for Urban Studies of MIT and Harvard University; Working Paper No. 19; February, 1973.

32. U.S. Bureau of the Census. *Census of Housing: 1970, Metropolitan Housing Characteristics.* Final Report HC(2)-146, Washington, D.C.: U.S. Government Printing Office, 1972.

33. U.S. Bureau of the Census. *Census of Population: 1970, Subject Reports, Migration Between State Economic Areas.* Final Report PC(2)-2E, Washington, D.C.: U.S. Government Printing Office, 1972.

34. U.S. Bureau of the Census. *Census of Population and Housing: 1970,*

Census Tracts. Final Report PHC(1)-142, Washington, D.C.: U.S. Government Printing Office, 1972.

35. U.S. Bureau of the Census. *Current Population Reports, Characteristics of the Population by Ethnic Origin: November, 1969.* Series P-20, No. 221, Washington, D.C.: U.S. Government Printing Office, 1971.

36. U.S. Bureau of the Census. *Current Population Reports, Demographic Projections for the U.S.* Series P-25, No. 476, Washington, D.C.: U.S. Government Printing Office, February 1972.

37. U.S. Bureau of the Census. *A Public Use Sample of Basic Records from the 1960 Census: Description and Technical Documentation.* Washington, D.C.: U.S. Government Printing Office, 1971.

38. U.S. Bureau of the Census. *U.S. Census of Population: 1960, Subject Reports, Mobility for States and State Economic Areas.* Final Report PC(2)-2B, Washington, D.C.: U.S. Government Printing Office, 1963.

39. U.S. Bureau of the Census. *U.S. Censuses of Population and Housing: 1960, Census Tracts.* Final Report PHC(1)-102, Washington, D.C.: U.S. Government Printing Office, 1961.

5 Real Estate

The prerequisite to developing a behaviorally based theory of New Haven's housing sector is a close look at the major activities taking place in what is conventionally called the real estate market. The earlier focus on neighborhood-to-neighborhood movements now is sharpened to the housing unit—to the whole matter of housing preferences, households bargaining with landlords and homeowners in the process of finding a place to live, and builders constructing new homes and apartments. And always in the picture are the effects of land use control on residential construction.

One of the first things New Haven's settlers did upon arriving in 1638 was to dig cellars in the ground along the West River to provide themselves with immediate shelter.[a] While living in these cellars, the settlers went about the business of building homes, the more substantial of which had clapboard siding and shingle roofs. The early settlers of New Haven paid no attention to the supposed American tradition of the log cabin; apparently they built New Haven's first homes with hand hewn lumber rather than with logs. The tradition of living in cellars, however, continued. Later settlers coming to New Haven often lived in the vacated cellars while they built their homes.

In the summer of 1638, the town was laid out in nine squares occupying in total a half square mile, with the center square reserved for public use as a marketplace and the other squares earmarked for residential and agricultural use. New Haven's present central business district occupies the area of the original town. The central square, now called "The New Haven Green," has never been developed and remains a public park in the center of the city.

Initially, as more settlers came, New Haven expanded from the original half square mile along the waterfront to the southwest in the Long Wharf area. Once the industrial growth of the early 19th century started, New Haven began to spread in all directions. The areas immediately to the west and south of the center, The Hill, Dwight and Dixwell, were largely developed as working class areas, characterized by small frame houses and tenaments, although a part of the Dwight area was developed in the middle of the 19th century with large homes for the wealthy. Wooster Square, to the east of the center, and the area adjacent to State Street to the north of the center were also developed in the early 19th century as working class areas. Until the early 20th century, when it was

[a]The material in this section has been obtained from Osterweis: *Three Centuries of New Haven, 1638-1938* [10] and The New Haven Community Renewal Program Study, *Residential Districts* [9].

overwhelmed by the growing public and business activity in the city center, "Quality Row," immediately to the north of the Green was the site of the elegant mansions of New Haven's leading citizens. As the city grew, most of the wealthy built their homes on Prospect Hill in the Whitney area to the north of Quality Row, creating a substantial and prosperous neighborhood between the working class areas to the east and west. The opening of the Farmington Canal in the 1820's brought industrial and residential development to Newhallville, north of Dixwell. The Olin and Winchester factories were built in Newhallville, and tenaments sprung up to house their workers. Development of the areas west of Dwight, Dixwell, and Newhallville largely occurred in the 20th century, and these areas are characterized mainly by single family homes in sound neighborhoods. Fair Haven, to the east of Wooster Square, developed in the middle of the 19th century, reamined a prosperous "suburb" until the early 1900's when industrial encroachment into the area signalled the decline of parts of Fair Haven as sound residential areas.

For the most part, the 19th century working class areas close to the center of the city, with their often poorly built tenements and close-packed triple deckers, became seriously declining sections of the city in the 20th century. In fact, even in the early 1800's, a section of Dixwell was known as "Poverty Square," and, apparently, much of the rest of Dixwell was not much better. Dixwell became one of New Haven's slums in the 20th century and a prime candidate for redevelopment by 1960. The Oak Street section in the central area of the city was probably New Haven's worst slum and was largely demolished to make way for the Oak Street Connector to the Connecticut Turnpike. The Hill, like Dixwell, developed with quickly and poorly-built structures, was in serious decline by the 1950's. Dwight, although a predominantly working class area, fared somewhat better; the housing built in the 19th century, although modest, was of reasonable quality. In the early part of this century considerable apartment construction occurred in the Dwight area, and many large homes there were converted to multi-family residences. Still, by the middle of this century Dwight was declining, as was Wooster Square, and to a lesser degree, portions of Fair Haven.

By 1960 New Haven city had evolved from a small half square mile town of a few hand-built homes in the wilderness, to an area of more than 22 square miles, developed with some 50,000 homes and apartments and with numerous stores, factories, and office buildings. The areas in the older parts of the city—Fair Haven, Wooster Square, Hill, Dwight, Dixwell, Newhallville—were characterized by old multi-unit structure housing and had seen virtually no development in the past 20 or 30 years. These areas, all declining, were (or were about to be) designated for various renewal projects. Most of the residential development in New Haven city during the 1950's occurred in the single-family sections largely on the western and eastern borders of the city.

Prior to 1920 the suburban areas of New Haven were the outer areas of the city itself. As growth continued in the city, the amount of vacant land available for building steadily diminished, and the wave of suburbanization passed beyond the city limits, particularly into West Haven, Hamden and East Haven. By 1960, most of the suburban areas adjacent to New Haven city—the western part of West Haven, the southern portion of Hamden, and the eastern sections of East Haven—were largely developed. With the exception of the parts of Hamden and West Haven close to the city, the housing in the suburban areas was predominately single-family housing, much of it less than ten years old. As can be seen from Table 5-1, most of the vacant land available for development in the metropolitan area was in the outlying towns of Orange, Woodbridge, Guilford, and in the northern sections of Hamden and North Haven.

Large amounts of undeveloped land at the periphery help to form a buffer zone between New Haven and adjacent regions. An enormous amount of population and business growth can be absorbed before New Haven runs short of land. Of the total land area of 129,000 acres in the New Haven SMSA in 1960, more than half (approximately 74,000 acres) was vacant and potentially available for future development, while only 31,000 acres were developed. It will in all probability be a long time before New Haven merges into Gottman's[b] megalopolis.

A closer look at housing in New Haven during the decade of the 1960's (see Table 5-2) reveals important shifts. First, the growth in the SMSA in the 1960's occurred in the suburbs. Secondly, the number of rental units in the suburbs

Table 5-1
1960 New Haven Land Use[1]

	Residential Use	*Commercial Ind. Use*	*Available Vacant*	*Unavailable[2]*	*Total*
New Haven City	4,908	1,915	1,112	4,337	12,272
Branford	2,441	382	8,606	2,566	13,995
East Haven	2,030	425	4,418	1,194	8,067
North Haven	2,502	535	7,802	2,087	12,926
Hamden	3,891	779	11,786	4,850	21,306
Woodbridge	2,254	25	8,125	1,840	12,244
Orange	2,814	311	6,879	1,113	11,117
West Haven	2,733	437	2,051	2,003	7,224
Guilford	2,180	212	23,161	4,675	30,228
Metropolitan Area	25,753	5,021	73,940	24,665	129,379

Source: Derived from Chase [3], Connecticut State Department of Transportation [4, 5], and Regional Planning Agency of South Central Connecticut [12].

[1]Areas given in acres.

[2]Land that is publically owned or otherwise unavailable for private development.

[b]See Gottman [7].

Table 5-2
Occupied Housing Units in the New Haven Central City, Suburbs, and Metropolitan Area, 1960 and 1970

	SMSA	*New Haven City*	*Suburbs*
Total Occupied Housing Units			
1960	95,515	49,170	46,345
1970	108,950	46,855	62,095
Owner-Occupied Units			
1960	53,601	16,573	37,028
1970	60,870	14,816	46,054
Renter-Occupied Units			
1960	41,914	32,597	9,317
1970	48,080	32,039	16,041
Percent Owner-Occupied			
1960	56.1%	33.7%	79.9%
1970	55.9%	31.6%	74.2%
Percent Renter-Occupied			
1960	43.9%	66.3%	20.1%
1970	44.1%	68.4%	25.8%

Source: Derived from U.S. Bureau of the Census [15, 17].

increased by approximately 75 percent. A third major change—the upward movement of rents and prices—will be discussed shortly.

Given the fact that New Haven city has not grown since 1920 and has been losing population since 1950, it is not surprising that all of the growth in the metropolitan area in the 1960's occurred in the suburban towns. As has already been mentioned, virtually all the vacant land in the New Haven area is located in the suburban towns, making it much easier and considerably less expensive to build new homes and apartments beyond the city limits. Thus, during the 1960's, the number of households in suburban towns taken together grew by 34 percent, while the number in the city decreased by 5 percent.

Substantial demolitions of both rental and owned units in the city, particularly in the early 1960's, helped in the reduction of the city's population and households, and of its housing stock. During the decade the city suffered a net loss of approximately 2,300 units.[c] At the same time, 5,500 new units were built in the city, replacing many of the estimated 7,800 units demolished. These

[c]The net loss of housing units in New Haven City is approximately equal to the decline in the number of occupied units since the number of vacant units in the city in 1970 was approximately the same as in 1960.

demolitions also helped to keep construction activity in the New Haven SMSA at a high level. Approximately 34 percent—7,800 units—of the 23,000 total new units coming onto the market between 1960 and 1970 replaced units demolished in the city. Without demolitions it is rather unlikely that construction activity would have led to significantly more than 14,000 new units—the increase in the number of households in the SMSA.[d]

As the suburbs were growing, the balance between renters and owners in the suburbs was changing. As Table 5-2 indicates, in 1960 about one out of every five occupied units in the suburbs was a rental unit; by 1970 the corresponding figure had increased to one out of every four. During the decade of the 1960's, the overall level of demand for rental units grew somewhat.[e] In addition an increasing number of renters preferred the suburbs over the city and thus provided the stimulus for more suburban rental construction.

The data in Table 5-3 suggest that the increase in suburban rental units was not shared uniformly by the eight suburban towns. West Haven accounted for 50 percent of the increase, and West Haven and Hamden together accounted for 74 percent of the new suburban rental units. Both Hamden, just to the north of the city, and West Haven, just to the west of the city, have large, well-developed areas adjacent to the city. For the most part, much of the new rental construction occurred in or near these built-up areas. In fact, by 1970 most of West Haven was largely developed and it had a sufficiently high concentration of renters (43 percent) to have lost its suburban character of ten years earlier. The remaining suburban areas are still occupied largely by people who own their homes.

The percentage of units built for rent increased substantially during the decade. In the early 1960's, new homes built for sale (mostly in the suburbs) accounted for 67 percent of all residential construction, compared with an average of 88 percent during the 1950's. By 1970, only 38 percent of new units built were for sale, and rental construction had reached a level of about 1,200 units a year—almost three times its level in 1960.[f]

---

[d]In the case of no demolitions, construction activity in excess of the increase in households leads to rising vacancy rates. As vacancy rates rise, construction will tend to decrease as builders attempt to keep their volume of building in balance with sales or rental rates.

[e]The New Haven area grew by 13,435 households during the 1960's. Rental occupancy increased by 6,166 households, or 46 percent of the total increase. Of all households in 1960, only 44 percent rented.

[f]It is interesting to note that the 1970 construction level of 740 units for sale approximately matches the estimated demand for owned units under the assumption that (1) the increase in households for the year is approximately 1,340 (the average yearly increase for the decade) and (2) the own/rent preference distribution of households at the margin is the same as the distribution for all households in the SMSA, so that approximately 56 percent—or 750—of the added households will become owners. This argument suggests that demolitions did not play a significant role in the for-sale market in the late 1960's and that the construction in excess of household increase occurred in the rental market.

Table 5-3
Occupied Housing Units in New Haven's Central City and Suburbs

	Owner-Occupied Units		*Renter-Occupied Units*	
	1960	*Change 1960-1970*	*1960*	*Change 1960-1970*
New Haven	16,573	−1,757	32,597	−558
Branford	3,607	949	1,488	520
East Haven	4,896	913	895	505
North Haven	4,103	1,676	346	155
Hamden	10,076	1,646	2,121	1,651
Woodbridge	1,281	647	144	167
Orange	2,254	1,330	149	36
West Haven	8,986	756	3,679	3,537
Guilford	1,825	1,108	496	154

Source: See Table 5-2

Another major shift in New Haven's housing sector during the 1960's was the change in rents and prices.[g] As can be seen from Table 5-4, the number of units in the high price and high rent categories[h] increased significantly.

The data in Table 5-4 indicate the strong upward pressure on rents and prices above and beyond the pressure of inflation. The column labelled "Change Due to Construction" gives an estimate (by price or rent) of new units added to the stock between 1960 and 1970. The column labelled "Change Due to Price/Rent Change" indicates the change in each price or rent category from causes other than new construction. For example, more than half of the total increase in high rent units was due to landlords raising rents of existing units in the face of strong demand and limited supply. It should be pointed out that the substantial demolition of rental units, largely in the low and medium rent range, occurring in New Haven city helped to deplete the rental supply. Also in some areas of the city many units were partially or totally renovated, and this improvement in housing quality often led to rent increases in the affected units. In addition to the rent movements illustrated by Table 5-4, there were substantial rent increases for rental units in the high rent category itself.

[g]By price we mean the estimated market price provided by the U.S. Census Bureau. By rent we mean the Census category "gross rent" which, for practical purposes, is equal to "actual" rent plus utilities.

[h]The price and rent categories in 1970 dollars are: High Price, greater than $33,000, Medium Price, $20,000 to $33,000, Low Price, less than $20,000; High Rent, greater than $130 per month, Medium Rent, $80 per month to $130 per month, and Low Rent, less than $80 per month. Inflation has been taken into account in the price and rent categories, so that, for example, in 1960 dollars the High Price range runs $25,000 and up, and the High Rent range runs $100 per month and up. According to the change in the Consumer Price Index, it took $1.31 in 1970 to buy goods and services costing $1.00 in 1960. Thus, to

Table 5-4
Price and Rent Levels in the New Haven Metropolitan Area, 1960 and 1970

	1960	*1970*	*Change*	*Change due to Construction*	*Change due to Price/Rent Change*
Owner-Occupied Units					
High Price	7,947	15,065	7,118	5,527	1,591
Medium Price	24,085	27,428	3,343	5,646	−2,303
Low Price	21,569	18,377	−3,192	805	−3,997
Renter-Occupied Units					
High Rent	8,056	25,252	17,196	8,121	9,075
Medium Rent	23,401	17,117	−6,284	1,231	−7,515
Low Rent	10,457	5,712	−4,745	824	−5,569

Source: Derived from U.S. Bureau of the Census [14, 15, 17].

The upward price push was also evident in the prices of newly constructed units for sale. At the beginning of the decade, close to 600 medium price units were built each year. This figure steadily dropped to 200 units by the end of the decade. At the same time the number of high price units built per year over the decade remained at the level of approximately 500 units. Thus the drop in for-sale construction between 1960 and 1970 is entirely associated with the decline in medium price construction. Rising costs of labor and materials, and particularly of land are responsible for this decline. In the rental market, high rent rental construction constituted approximately 90 percent of all rental construction throughout the decade.

The pattern of rent and price shifts in the city and the suburbs differed quite substantially. Virtually all the appreciation of home values occurred in the suburbs, reflecting the fact that the great bulk of demand for owned units was focused on the suburbs. Most of the rental increases in the suburbs occurred within the high rent category, while in the city the biggest shift in rents was caused by medium rent units being pushed up into the high rent category.

In summary, a variety of changes occurred in the New Haven housing sector during the 1960's. An increasing number of rental units were being built outside the central city, and an increasing number of all units built were rental units. A more detailed look at the suburbs indicates that most of the new suburban rental units were located in the more developed, large suburban towns of Hamden and West Haven. There were strong increases in rents and less dramatic appreciation of home values, each showing different locational patterns. The purpose of our analysis of the real estate market is to explain these changes.

correct for inflation, we have multiplied the 1960 price/rent categories boundaries by 1.31 to arrive at the 1970 categories.

Dynamics of the Real Estate Market

Our discussion of the real estate market is orgainzed around three major phenomena: (1) households choosing housing and negotiating a rent or price to be paid with the landlord or owner, (2) construction of new units, and (3) towns imposing land use controls. Attention focuses primarily on the actions and decisions of the people who participate in this market. We consider landlords, homeowners selling their houses, builders, bankers, and zoning board members. Each of these people plays a major role in the real estate market, and each influences the activities of the others. A family buying a home buys it from another family, or a builder, and, typically, borrows money from a mortgage banker in the process. Rents and prices are determined by the bargaining between prospective tenants and landlords, and prospective buyers and home owners. The supply of available housing in a particular area is determined by the number of households moving out of that area and by the rate of new construction and demolition. The housing choices of households influence builders when they decide how many units to build and where to build them. The results of these interconnected actions and decisions are the "phenomena" of the real estate market—the construction of new units, changes in prices and rents, changes in land use. It seems reasonable to suppose that if we can begin to understand the reasoning and motivation behind the decisions made by builders, landlords and others in the real estate market, we are well along the way toward being able to formulate a predictive, behaviorally based theory of real estate phenomena.

An important ingredient is the choice of housing categories or types. We have categorized housing according to whether the unit is owned or rented, that is, by its tenure type rather than by structure type. Although most rental units are in multi-unit structures, and most owned homes are single-family structures, the correspondence between structure type and tenure is not one-to-one. The choice of tenure, whether to rent or to buy, is among the most fundamental choices a household makes when looking for housing and thus should be explicitly considered in a behaviorally oriented theory. During the 1960's, it turns out to be quite reasonable to suppose that all new units built for sale were single-family structures, and that all new rental units were in multi-unit structures. However, with the rise in popularity of condominiums,[i] it appears to be the case that an increasing number of new units for sale in the 1970's will be in multi-unit structures.[j]

Prices and rents are clearly important from a behavioral point of view; owners selling their homes, for example, are vitally concerned with the price they will

---

[i]A household living in a condominium owns the housing unit itself, but shares ownership of the common areas of the building and the land on which the building is located with the other inhabitants of the structure.

[j]It is beyond the scope of our model to deal with multi-unit structures in an explicit manner.

get. We use ranges rather than a median to categorize prices and rents because three price and three rent categories contain significantly more information than do a median price and a median rent.

Occupying a House

Once the household has narrowed down the choice of neighborhoods and begins to talk with landlords or real estate agents about renting or buying a specific housing unit, an interesting chain of events begins.

Choosing a Unit. The first thing that must be established is who wants what. The "joint" characteristics of households are central to the theory of housing preferences. In particular, the patterns of occupancy, illustrated in Table 5-5 for the case of young, native households, contain a great deal of information about what types of housing units these households prefer. The entry in the left-most upper box, for example, is the number of young, native households with less than a high school education who live in high price homes. From Table 5-5 we can infer that most young native households with less than a high school education will prefer to rent, that young, native households with more than a high school education will have a stronger preference for high price homes than do their counterparts with a high school education.

In general, the propensity of a household to own increases with the household head's level of education, as does the propensity to live in more expensive housing. Most of the low price and low rent housing in 1960 was occupied by households with heads having less than a high school education.

Table 5-5
Occupancy Patterns of Young, Native Households in 1960

	Type of Unit Occupied						
	Own			*Rent*			
Household Type (young, native)	*High Price*	*Medium Price*	*Low Price*	*High Rent*	*Medium Rent*	*Low Rent*	*Total*
Less than High School Education	67	1,710	2,502	643	3,508	1,329	9,759
High School Education	300	2,319	2,036	326	2,136	504	7,621
More than High School Education	1,385	2,501	911	1,426	1,591	248	8,062
TOTAL	1,752	6,530	5,449	2,395	7,235	2,081	25,442

Source: Derived from U.S. Bureau of the Census [16,17].

Most of the high price and high rent housing was occupied by households with heads having more than a high school education. The propensity of middle-aged and old households to own is generally higher than that of young households, and a somewhat greater percentage of middle-aged households own than do old households. In a given age and education bracket, the percentage of minority households that own is considerably less than that of their native and foreign counterparts, reflecting discrimination in the real estate market and the fact of the generally lower economic status of minorities.

Households who move within the New Haven area (or move into it from outside the area) do not have precisely the same housing preferences as does the corresponding population as a whole. In the first place, in-migrants are much more likely to look for a rental unit, if for no other reason than to have a convenient base from which to look for a house to buy. In the second place, renters are far more mobile than home owners, by a factor of about 5 to 1 in the New Haven area. Most renters, when they move will rent again.[k] Thus the population of movers has a greater propensity to rent than does the population at large. Finally, many movers will be moving to upgrade their housing as well as their neighborhood, and will tend to prefer higher price housing than the population at large. The housing preferences of each type of household moving into or within the SMSA reflect these basic differences.[l]

We assume for the most part that the housing preferences of households at the joint level change slowly with time; that is, that the preferences in 1980 will be much the same as they were in 1960. We see little reason to suppose, for example, that an affluent family with children, will not continue to prefer, in all probability, to own a high-priced home.

The level of demand for rental units increased during the 1960's. This shift is attributable not so much to a shift in preferences, however, as to an increase in the proportion of households with higher propensities to rent. The demand for and construction of rental units consequently grew. In addition, and of growing importance, is the price squeeze in owned housing indicated by the decline in construction of medium price units. As house prices rise, medium income households will find it increasingly hard to buy a home and will be forced to rent. These households will not be able to meet the mortgage banker's criteria that a person's house should be valued at no more than two and one half times his income.

At the tract level, the number and type of available vacant units play an important role in neighborhood selection and housing choice.[m] The unit a

---

[k]See Pack [11].

[l]For example, from Table 5-5, 43.8 percent of all young native households with less than a high school education are owners. However, only 27.7 percent of movers of this type buy homes.

[m]For example, the number of households that move into a tract is limited by the number of available vacant units in that tract. A discussion of how we impose this constraint and

household finally occupies will depend on the balance of their preferences with the reality of the real estate market. The reality is, of course, that the supply of available housing is limited and that prices and rents are constantly rising. In the next section we discuss the bargaining between households and owners or landlords to establish prices and rents, and to determine who will occupy the available housing.

Bargaining for Housing. There are no hard and fast rules to determine the price a selling owner should ask for his house or the rent a landlord should ask for a vacant apartment. It is not unusual to find, in any neighborhood, a home that has been on the market for a long time because, as real estate agents will tell you, the asking price is too high. The agent will assert that if the house were priced "realistically," it would sell quickly. A landlord who raises the rent of an available unit substantially may realize that the raise is too high if the unit remains vacant for an extended time. The intitial asking price or rent of an available housing unit is determined by guesswork. The landlord or owner must guess what he thinks the market will bear. If his guess is a good one, his unit will soon be occupied. If his guess is a bad one, the unit will not be sold or rented quickly, and he may very well have to lower the asking price or rent to attract business. Sometimes rather than actually lower the monthly rent itself, landlords will instead offer one or two months of free occupancy to prospective tenants.

In our theory of the bargaining process[n] we assume that an owner selling his home will ask for a higher price than he paid and that a landlord with an available rental unit will ask for more rent than he got from the previous tenant. Thus, for example, some of the vacant, medium rent units that were previously occupied become high rent units. Once the initial asking prices and rents have been set, the prospective occupants are ready to make their bids. If the number of households wanting high rent units is less than the number of available high rent units, then these households reach agreement with the landlords and occupy the units. If there are a substantial number of vacant high rent units left after those bidding for high rent units have taken occupancy, some of these vacant units will drop to the medium range as the landlords attempt to lower rents to make the units more attractive to the remaining bidders. Similarly, some of their available medium rent units left vacant after the bidding may have their rents lowered to the low rent range.

The outcome of the bargaining determines who moves into what unit, and how many and what types of units will remain vacant. The level of vacant units gives a measure of the balance between supply and demand in the real estate market and is of great importance to builders, to whose role we now turn.

"clear" the real estate market is found in Birch, Atkinson, Sandström and Stack [2], Section VI.

[n]For a more detailed discussion of how this theory is implemented, see Birch, Atkinson, Sandström, and Stack [2], Section VI.

Construction

In simple terms, the level of residential construction is determined by the fact that builders are in business to make a profit. If they can sell at a reasonable profit they will stay in business. If not, they will fold. In particular, if vacancy rates go up in a neighborhood where new units are being built, construction activity will decrease. Rising vacancy rates in such a neighborhood are the signal that more units are being built than the market will bear and indicate that builders are holding stocks of unsold homes or unrented apartments. The interest costs of construction loans are high enough that few builders can afford to carry such an inventory for long. Usually they are forced to sell out—often at a loss—within a few months. Thus, as much as possible, a builder will attempt to match his rate of construction to the rate of anticipated sales in order to keep his balance of vacant units at a reasonable level.

Any analysis of construction must distinguish between the decisions made by builders of rental units and builders of units for sale. There are considerable differences between the financing, planning and operational patterns of apartment and single-family builders. Often a builder will specialize exclusively in one or the other of these two distinct markets. The single-family home builder can proceed unit-by-unit and has rather close control of his inventory of unsold units. He can easily operate on a "sell-one-start-one" basis. An apartment builder, on the other hand, cannot easily operate on a "rent-one-start-one" basis. For one thing, he cannot, for practical purposes, guide the day-to-day construction work of an individual apartment building in response to market conditions. His planning problems, often involving lead times of two to three years, are in general far more complex than those of a single-family builder. Typically, a single-family unit can be constructed in two to three months. The rental market often tends to be more volatile than the for-sale market, partly because of the high rates of renter mobility, partly because of the sometimes speculative nature of apartment construction financing. As a consequence, acceptable vacancy levels in the rental market are higher than in the owned home market. A 5 percent vacancy rate indicates a reasonable balance in the rental market in New Haven. Such a vacancy rate in the owned market would lead to a substantial reduction in for-sale construction.

Another important characteristic of the residential construction industry is the fact that the industry is highly fragmented with many competing builders and financial institutions. It is often the case that individual builders work in relatively well-defined geographical and price/rent segments of the market. For the most part, those active in the supply side of the real estate market—builders, real estate agents, landlords and so on—tend to focus largely on conditions in their local market area. In order to capture this aspect of the real estate market, as it pertains to construction activity, each geographical and price/rent market segment must be treated in a largely individual fashion.

The decision rules followed by the "average" builder in each market segment are formulated in terms of an answer to the question: "This year should I increase or decrease my number of starts?" A builder, on the basis of his past sales and expectations for future sales, may decide to decrease his activity 10 percent over last year or, in other circumstances, decide to decrease construction by 5 percent. A graph of a typical decision rule is shown in Figure 5-1. As the vacancy rate increases past a maximum trigger rate, the builder will decrease construction. Once vacancy rates fall below a minimum vacancy rate, he will start up again.

As already mentioned, there are separate decision rules for each market segment. The form of the decision rule is the same for each tract, reflecting the fact that builders in different areas of the SMSA tend to operate by the same kind of rules. For example, the minimum and maximum vacancy trigger rates (0.3 percent and 3.0 percent respectively) are the same for high price for-sale builders in all tracts. If vacancy rates are increasing, say, in North Haven, and decreasing in Orange, building is likely to decrease in North Haven and to increase in Orange. A builder in a particular segment of the market will tend to make his decision on the basis of the state of his portion of the market.

The major exception to the treatment of construction on an individual tract-by-tract, type-by-type basis is caused by excess demand. Excess demand is a measure of the number of households, broken down by type of unit preferred, who want to move into a tract but who cannot get in due to lack of available housing. A tract in which there are waiting lists for new apartment projects is a good example of a tract with excess rental demand. Builders respond speculatively under these conditions, particularly in a tight rental market. High rent rental builders seem to increase their building rates if there is excess high rent rental demand in any tract where rental construction is permitted. In New Haven there appears to be no instance of a large speculative increase in medium rent construction.

Land Use

Construction cannot occur when there is no vacant land available for building.[o] As land becomes more expensive, single-family construction becomes less and less economically feasible. An often used rule of thumb is that the land cost should not exceed 20 percent of the total cost of a new single-family home. Thus, for example, in an area where building lots are selling for \$6,000, new home prices will typically be at least \$30,000. Land prices increase as the

[o]An obvious exception is construction on land that has been cleared through the demolition of previous structures. This type of construction is handled exogenously in the simulation model.

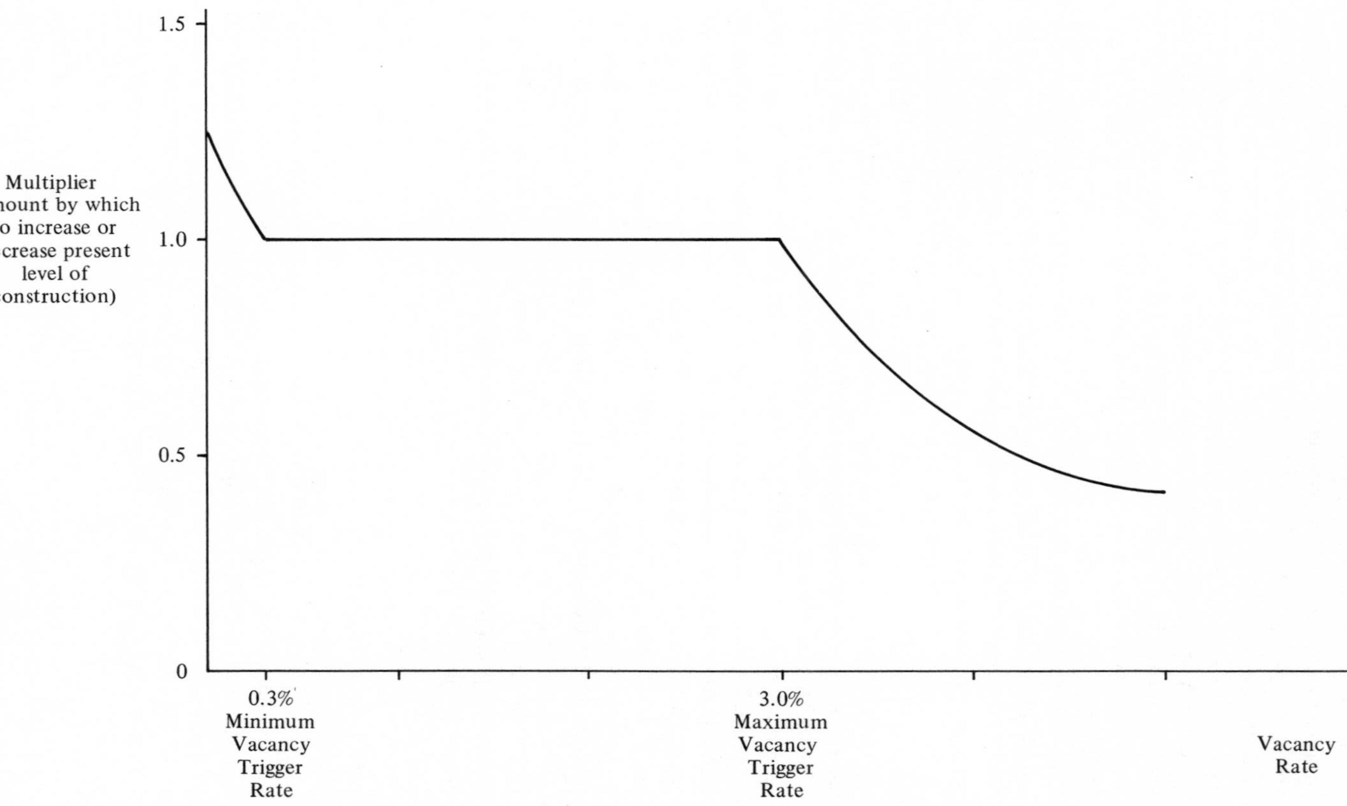

Figure 5-1 For-Sale Builder Decision Rule

density of development in a tract increases. As land in a tract becomes scarcer and more expensive, single-family high price and especially medium price home construction in that tract will decrease. By 1970, there were few areas within the New Haven SMSA where lots could be found on which it was economically feasible to build medium price, single-family homes.

Land Use Controls. There are in the New Haven SMSA a number of areas, the town of Orange being one good example, in which rental construction is prohibited or severly limited through the imposition of land-use controls. Yet, there is a clear and increasing demand for rental units in these areas. The question is: Will the prohibitions or controls be relaxed in future years? Changes in land-use controls must be understood in order to predict future construction. Unfortunately, as Grace Milgram[p] has observed, "one of the surprising gaps in economic knowledge is the absence of a well-developed body of theory and inventory of empirical data relating to urban land." Because virtually no quantitative theory of land use control could be found, such a theory had of necessity to be developed mainly from qualitative sources of information and from observation of land use patterns in New Haven.

Our major interest is in the processes by which land-use controls change. The two primary ingredients causing change appear to be shifts in the composition of the population of a town and the pressure of economic interests—primarily developers and landowners. Different types of people have different views on what constitutes an appropriate pattern of land use, and as the population changes, the political pressures on zoning boards change. The importance of economic forces has been stressed by the American Society of Planning Officials in their report, *Problems of Zoning and Land-Use Regulations:*

Nevertheless, almost from the day the zoning ordinance is adopted, the forces of the market will start eroding and changing the (land-use) plan. The owner of land in an industrial area declares he cannot sell his land for industry, but he does have an offer if it can be used for a shopping center. The owner of single-family residential land says there is no market for single family homes and he must therefore be permitted to build apartments. City councils find such arguments convincing.[q]

At any particular time, land-use controls reflect a balance between the political power the local population can muster to enforce its desires and the political and economic power of developers who wish to develop vacant land in the area.

Further support for the importance of economic forces in land-use control is given by Bernard Siegan in his book *Land Use Without Zoning*[r], a study of land

[p]See Milgram [8].

[q]See American Society of Planning Officials [1].

[r]See Siegan [13].

use controls in Houston, the sole major metropolitan area without zoning. Among his conclusions are:

> Economic forces tend to make for a separation of uses even without zoning. Business uses will tend to locate in certain areas, residential in others, and industrial in still others. Apartments will tend to concentrate in certain areas and not in others. There is also a tendency for further separation within a category; light industrial uses do not want to adjoin heavy industrial uses, and vice-versa. Different kinds of business uses require different locations. Expensive homes will separate from less expensive ones, townhouses, duplexes, etc. It is difficult to assess the effectiveness of zoning in furthering this process. It is more successful in this respect in the "bedroom" suburbs, but much less so in the larger cities. However, pressures may develop under zoning leading to greater proliferation of uses.
>
> A nonzoned city is a cosmopolitan collection of property uses. The standard is supply and demand, and if there is economic justification for the use, it is likely to be forthcoming. Zoning restricts the supply of some uses, and thereby prevents some demands from being satisfied. It may likewise impede innovation. In general, however, zoning in the major cities, which contain diverse life styles, probably has responded and accommodated to most consumer demands. This has not occurred usually in the more homogeneous suburbs.

In the spirit of Siegan's comments, we can say that zoning probably does little more than slow down the inevitable.

Changes in land-use control can be traced to the political process underlying the imposition of zoning or sub-division ordinances or whatever form the controls take. As far as residential construction is concerned, prohibitions, or relaxation of prohibitions, against rental construction are critical. If the residents of an area vote a sufficiently high maximum allowable residential density, developers will move in and build apartments. On the other hand, if the residents vote for a residential density comparable with single-family housing densities (up to 4 or 5 units per acre), apartment construction will be prohibited, or severely limited.

In order to determine the land-use control voting patterns, the characteristics of households in tracts where significant numbers of rental units were built during the 1960's were compared with the characteristics of households in tracts where rental construction was highly limited. Three distinct classes of households emerge: those who vote strongly in favor of rental unit construction, those who vote strongly in favor of severely limiting rental construction, and those who vote for a moderate amount of rental construction. The most predominate types strongly in favor of rental construction are young native households with less than a high school education, and foreign born households with less than a high school education. Those in favor of a moderate degree of rental construction are middle-aged and old native households with less than a high school education and young native households with a high school education. Those most strongly opposed to rental construction are young and middle-aged native households with more than a high school education who own their homes. In short, the higher the propensity of a household type to be a renter, the more likely it is that household type will be in favor of rental construction.

In determining the influence of economic forces, properties of the tracts themselves are important. Many apartment complexes, for example, are built on land that is unsuitable for building single family homes, either because the land itself is inherently hard to build on, or because it is adjacent to strip developments or shopping centers or major transportation arteries. Often, areas of apartment buildings form a buffer between commercially used land and single family residential areas. Because jobs are treated at the district level in our simulation, it is impossible to determine whether, for example, growth in service or retail jobs in a particular tract (to be discussed in the next chapter) is taking place in scattered areas or is the result of a new shopping center being developed.[s] As a proxy for service and retail job concentration, we have used the percentage of developed land in a tract devoted to service and retail jobs. It appears that a tract that has more than 10 percent of its developed land devoted to retail and service jobs and that, in addition, has more than a third of its vacant land in the hard to build category (vacant land that is characterized by steep slope, poor drainage, etc.) is much more likely to be attractive to rental builders than a tract that does not have these two characteristics.

In an area attractive to rental builders where there are strong limitations against rental building, builders will attempt through political and economic means to change the limitations. The higher the builders perceive the potential rental demand for that area to be, the harder they will try to obtain a change in land-use controls. Thus, if the excess demand for rental units in a tract is high and the tract has a sufficient amount of its developed land devoted to retail and service jobs and a sufficient amount of its vacant land is in the hard-to-build category, then the voting "power" of households who vote for more than five units per acre increases, reflecting the pressure of market forces in the land-use control process.

Predictive Accuracy

As in the preceding chapter, we are interested in the average errors between the predictions of the model and the actual data. Table 5-6 presents the average errors between simulated results and actual data in the case of a run from 1960 and 1967. The table includes, as well, our estimates of the accuracy of the data.[t]

---

[s]The technique used to allocate district-level jobs to individual tracts is discussed in Birch, Atkinson, Sandström and Stack [2], Section VII.

[t]In the case of housing, there are six individual joints—high price own, high rent, and so

Table 5-6
Average Percent Error for Occupied Housing Stock in 1967 for 1960-1967 Run and Estimated Accuracy of 1967 Data

		Simulated vs. Actual		
		Totals	*Marginals*	*Joints*
Occupied Housing Stock	SMSA	0.1%	0.9%	1.6%
	District	2.5%	6.8%	12.4%
	Tract	4.2%	9.5%	16.0%
		Uncertainty in "Actuals"		
		Totals	*Marginals*	*Joints*
Estimated Accuracy of the 1967 data for Occupied Housing Stock	SMSA	±1.0%	±2.0%	± 5.0%
	District	±3.0%	±5.0%	±10.0%
	Tract	±5.0%	±9.0%	±20.0%

In most cases our "predictions" for 1967 fall with the range of error of the actual data, as is also the case when we run to 1970.

In reaching this level of accuracy, our simulation of New Haven's real estate market during the 1960's "predicts" the growth of overall rental demand, the strong rise in the amount of rental construction, and the decrease in medium price construction. Most of the new suburban rental units "built in the model" are built in West Haven and Hamden. Appreciation of home values is strongest in the suburbs, and rents rise sharply in the city.

Summary

Our model of the real estate market, based on behavioral considerations, is reasonably successful in replicating the history of housing in New Haven during the 1960's. We anticipate that many trends of the 1960's will continue into the 1970's. The suburbs will continue to grow, more rental units will be built in the suburbs, and prices and rents will continue to rise. An aspect of housing our model does not capture that will be important in the 1970's is the rise of the condominium and other forms of higher density owned homes.

Much has been written about the "counter-intuitiveness"[u] of complex systems, and the housing sector of an urban area is indeed a complex system. We feel, however, that the real estate market, when viewed through the eyes of

on–which may be arranged in a 2 x 3–tenure x price/rent–table. There are five individual marginals–total renter occupied, high price plus high rent occupied, and so on–obtained by summing the table by rows and columns.

[u]See Forrester [6].

participants, is in actual practice quite "intuitive;" that is, actors in the real estate market proceed by reasonably well-defined rules, and exhibit considerable regularity. If our work indicated, for example, a spurt of single-family home construction in the central city in response to virtually any stimulus, we would say that we had produced a "counter-intuitive" result. The only way the real estate market could become "counter-intuitive" is for households to change their housing preferences in a radical fashion or for real estate agents, or builders, or bankers, to change their basic patterns of operation. We see little indication that any of those events will happen, and see instead a future that is quite consistent with our intuition based on the past.

Our theory rests on four rather intuitive notions:

1. The housing preferences of households are closely related to the patterns of occupancy.
2. Landlords and homeowners selling their homes will attempt to get the highest rent or price possible.
3. As long as builders can sell what they build and can avoid large inventories of vacant units, they will continue to build new housing units, otherwise not.
4. Land prices and land-use controls strongly influence the price and geographical composition of construction, and are, in turn, influenced by the "politics" of the local community in which the land is found.

The work of developing a detailed model is largely concerned with formulating these notions in quantitative terms and embedding them in a structure that allows them to interact with each other.

References

1. American Society of Planning Officials. *Problems of Zoning and Land Use Regulation.* National Commission on Urban Problems, Research Report No. 2. Washington, D.C.: U.S. Government Printing Office, 1968.

2. Birch, David L., Reilly Atkinson, Sven Sandström, Linda Stack. *The New Haven Laboratory.* Lexington, Mass.: Lexington Books, D.C. Heath & Co., 1974.

3. Chase, Bradford. *Vacant Land Characteristics.* Staff Paper No. 231, Hartford, Conn.: Connecticut Regional Planning Program, 1965.

4. Connecticut State Department of Transportation. *1970 Land Use Tabulations.* Hartford, Conn.: State of Connecticut, 1972.

5. Connecticut State Department of Transportation. *1964 Vacant Land Tabulations.* Hartford, Conn.: State of Connecticut, 1964.

6. Forrester, Jay W., *Urban Dynamics.* Cambridge, Mass.: The MIT Press, 1969.

7. Gottman, Jean. *Megalopolis: The Urbanized Northeastern Seaboard of the United States.* Cambridge, Mass.: The MIT Press, 1967.

8. Milgram, G. *U.S. Land Prices–Directions and Dynamics.* National Commission on Urban Problems, Research Report No. 13. Washington D.C.: Government Printing Office, 1968.

9. New Haven Community Renewal Program. *Residential Districts.* New Haven, 1964.

10. Osterweis, R.G. *Three Centuries of New Haven.* New Haven: Yale University Press, 1953.

11. Pack, Janet. *Movers Survey: Some Dimensions of the Housing Market of the City of New Haven.* New Haven City Planning Department, 1969.

12. Regional Planning Agency of South Central Connecticut. *1960 Land Use Tabulations.* Unpublished Census Tract Tabulations, early 1960's.

13. Siegan, Bernard H. *Land Use Without Zoning.* Lexington, Mass.: Lexington Books, D.C. Heath & Co., 1972.

14. U.S. Bureau of the Census. *Census of Housing: 1970, Metropolitan Housing Characteristics.* Final Report HC(2)–146, Washington, D.C.: U.S. Government Printing Office, 1972.

15. U.S. Bureau of the Census. *Census of Population and Housing: 1970, Census Tracts.* Final Report PHC(1)–142, Washington, D.C.: U.S. Government Printing Office, 1972.

16. U.S. Bureau of the Census. *A Public Use Sample of Basic Records from the 1960 Census: Description and Technical Documentation.* Washington, D.C.: U.S. Government Printing Office, 1971.

17. U.S. Bureau of the Census. *U.S. Censuses of Population and Housing: 1960, Census Tracts.* Final Report PHC(1)–102, Washington, D.C.: U.S. Government Printing Office, 1961.

6 Jobs

Throughout its history, the growth of the New Haven metropolitan area and the well-being of its residents have been closely tied to its economy and the roles its business firms and organizations have chosen to play. The purpose of this chapter is to take a closer look at the New Haven economy and its major actors—the manufacturer, the trucker, the grocery store owner, the blue collar worker, the self-employed professional, the shopper, and so forth.

Earlier we traced developments in New Haven's manufacturing sector. The ventures of such people as Eli Whitney, Samuel Colt, John Marlin, Oliver Winchester, Isacc Strouse, Max Adler, Joseph Sargent, Charles Goodyear, John Cook, and James Brewster were chronicled. Many names could be added to this list of people who caused the rapid expansion of New Haven during the period from 1840 to 1920.[a] The above mentioned are the most important and give the general picture: the inventive and entrepreneurial spirit found in New Haven during the first half of the 19th century led to the formation of an advanced technological and organizational base which enabled New Haven to prosper and expand rapidly for three quarters of a century. But it appears as though New Haven had "run out of steam" by the end of World War I. The pioneers were gone, and few had stepped in to take their place. New technologies and new products were developed in other cities, and New Haven's growth tapered off.

New Haven has also been well represented in transportation, trade, services, and education. Figure 6-1 shows how these tertiary industries[b] have grown in importance in the U.S. in the last hundred years, expanding their share of total employment from 25 percent in 1870 to 70 percent in 1970. Many of our presently largest metropolitan centers managed to take advantage of this growth pattern, New York being a prime example with its concentration of trade and communications activities. But why did New Haven not get a larger share of this growth? In trade, for instance, Boston and New York were able to establish themselves as important trade centers early, and New Haven has never overcome the head start of those two cities. The port of New Haven had only a brief period of expansion and prosperity, beginning shortly after the signing of the peace treaty with the British in 1783 and ending with the institution of embargo policies in 1807. The port never quite recovered after the embargo and the War

[a]This section draws primarily on Osterweis's history of New Haven [13].

[b]Agriculture, forestry, fisheries, and mining are usually referred to as primary industries, manufacturing as secondary, and all others as tertiary industries.

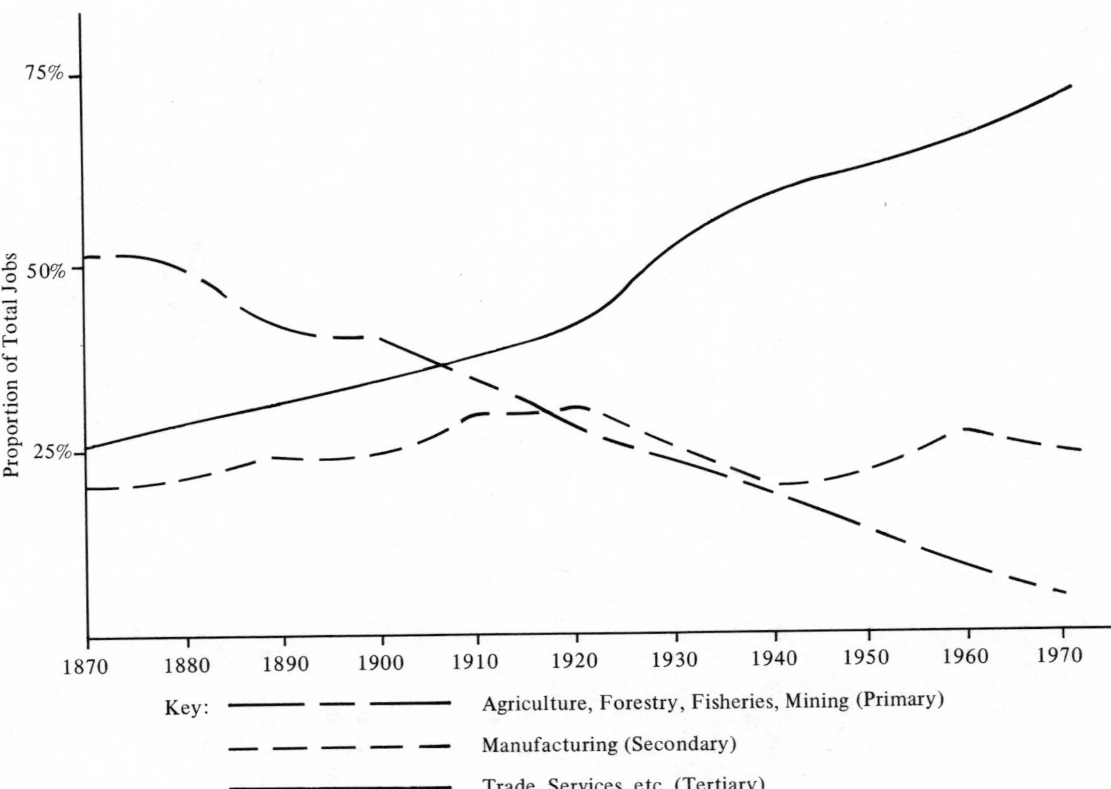

Figure 6-1 The Proportion of U.S. Jobs in Primary, Secondary and Tertiary Industries, 1870 to 1970

of 1812. Contributing to its difficulties was the British decision to dump accumulated surplus hardware and textiles in New York after the War, thereby furthering the growth of national wholesale markets in that city to the relative disadvantage of New Haven.

Good connections with the interior could have given impetus to the development of New Haven as a trade center. When the value to New York of the Erie Canal became evident in the late 1810's, work began on a canal system (including the Farmington Canal) linking New Haven with the interior of Connecticut and Massachusetts. By 1835 the work was completed, but the system never had the expected impact on New Haven because of competition from alternative transport routes and modes as well as lack of financial support from the state. The New Haven railroads were also plagued with many problems of fragmentation and mistakes in the timing of construction when they were developed in the mid-19th century. The consolidation of the railroads at the end of the century, their increased efficiency, and the construction of highways during this century helped New Haven to preserve its relative trade position, but it was too late to hope for any dramatic improvements. The trade patterns were already established.

Turning to the service-related industries, we find New Haven in a rather promising position. Banks, insurance companies, hotels, repair shops, movie houses, the medical and legal professions are included in these industries. Up until rather recently most of them were not specialized, and catered to the local population rather than to a wider market. They were not the driving forces behind the growth of a city in the same way as manufacturing and, to a certain extent, trade were. This is changing. The economy is becoming more and more "human capital" oriented. The degree of specialization in the service sectors is rapidly increasing, and the markets are becoming distance independent. New Haven may well be on the verge of a new period of growth and prosperity. Its situation today may be similar to that of 1840, except that the source of its growth may be humanly and socially oriented instead of being based on physical production. Yale University, with its excellent professional schools, will play an important role. One hundred years after its founding in 1701, Yale was the largest institution of higher learning in the nation. The most rapid expansion has, however, occurred over the last forty years, and its student body now approaches 10,000. With 7,000 employees, Yale is the largest employer in the area.

Before attempting a more detailed analysis of the development between 1960 and 1970, let us introduce an additional dimension into the picture: the spatial one. So far we have largely neglected the location of jobs within the SMSA, an aspect of urban change on which we shall concentrate in the following sections. The limited data that exist for the period prior to 1960 reveal two interesting facts. First, both manufacturing and other jobs have been very concentrated in the city. In 1960, for instance, only 48 percent of the SMSA population lived in the city while 65 percent of the manufacturing jobs and 70 percent of all other jobs were located there (see Figure 6-2). Second, the central city share of manufacturing jobs is decreasing much more rapidly than its share of the population. Its share of non-manufacturing jobs is, however, decreasing at about the same rate as its share of the population. The dramatic shift of manufacturing jobs from the central city to the suburbs started in the 1950's, and from 1960 to 1967 the central city's share of manufacturing jobs dropped from 65 percent to 48 percent. Later in this chapter we shall discuss how and why this shift took place.

Continuing to the next level of description–where the jobs were located within the city itself–we first have to stress what has implicitly been said several times in earlier chapters: people went where the jobs went. The location of the Winchester factory in Newhallville, for instance, not far from the old Whitney plant in Hamden, resulted in the settlement of its employees in this and surrounding neighborhoods, particularly Dixwell. Later, many other industries moved to this area, causing new waves of residential construction. The early concentration of workers-cum-residents in this part of the city also attracted many retail stores (grocery and hardware stores, for instance) and service businesses (barber shops, bars, and so forth). Today we find a significant proportion of the city's automotive services concentrated here, particularly along Whalley Avenue. This is an example of an urban development process in which the manufacturers–in this case men like Eli Whitney and Oliver Winchester–were the key decision-makers. Their decisions on where to build plants determined the future of the area.

But why did these districts attract the manufacturers in the first place? Several main thoroughfares, such as Whitney and Dixwell and Whalley Avenues, were laid out at the turn of the 19th century, pointing from the center of the city towards the north and northwest and directing attention and growth in that direction. Yale was thriving just north of the center, in the Whitney district. Furthermore, the Farmington Canal was constructed along the boundary between Whitney to the east and Newhallville, Dixwell and Dwight to the west, which increased the attractiveness of these districts. Later the conversion of the canal into a railroad helped to maintain the manufacturer' interest in the area.

Two other city districts that proved to be good locations for manufacturing were Long Wharf and Fair Haven. Fair Haven's main attraction was originally Mill River and later the railroad which defines its boundary with the Whitney District. Today Interstate Route 91 provides good transportation connections for firms located in the western part of the district. A large number of manufacturers are also located on the other side of the railroad tracks and along the interstate route in the Whitney area. Long Wharf, which includes the bulk of New Haven's port facilities, did not exert as much attraction on manufacturers as one might have expected. This is mostly due to the low importance of the port in the early years of New Haven manufacturing and the successful

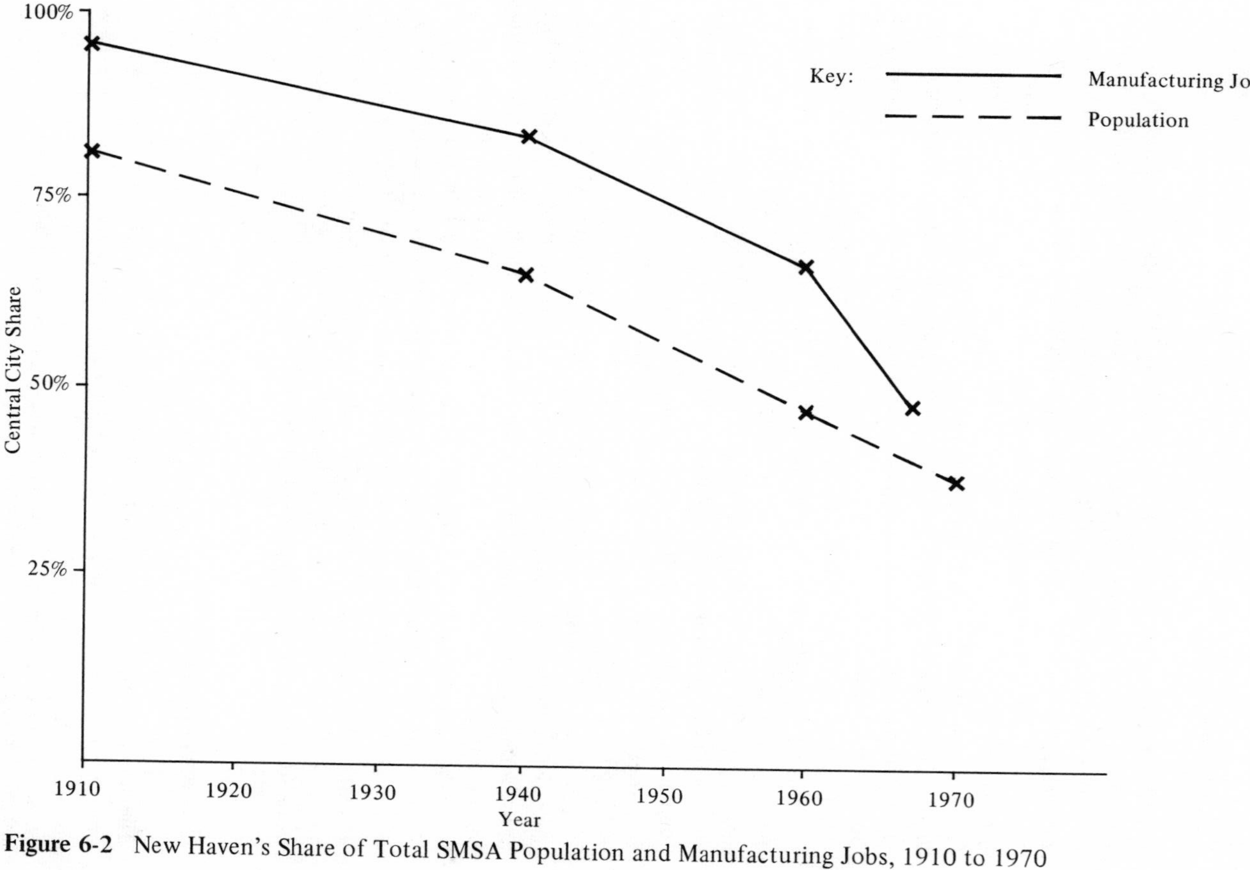

Figure 6-2 New Haven's Share of Total SMSA Population and Manufacturing Jobs, 1910 to 1970

competition from the canal and later the railroads and highways. Still, some 10 percent of the city's manufacturing jobs could be found in Long Wharf in 1960.

A Closer Look at 1960-1967

A more detailed look at the 1960 to 1967 period lends some support to our analysis of the long-term aspects of New Haven's development and our prediction of future trends. Table 6-1 provides data on employment structure and growth in the U.S. and in the New Haven SMSA between 1960 and 1967.[c] Despite the many jobs generated in the SMSA because of the Vietnam war, total manufacturing jobs increased at a much lower rate than for the nation as a whole. From 1960 to 1967 the proportion of manufacturing jobs to total jobs went down from 36 percent to 32 percent while it remained constant at 26 percent for the nation. That is, the area's specialization in manufacturing vis-à-vis the nation decreased.

The trend was the opposite for jobs in the fast-growing finance, insurance, services and government industries where New Haven's growth was much higher than the nation's, 37 percent versus 28 percent. The fact that New Haven is reducing its dependence on manufacturing and switching its employment to more rapidly growing sectors suggests that we can expect New Haven's population and employment to grow at a higher rate in the future than they have over the last few decades. A revival of New Haven may be on its way, as was suggested earlier.

There was, of course, considerable variation in growth rates within the various parts of the SMSA, as indicated in Table 6-2 where the 1960-1967 growth has been broken down by city and suburbs. The sharp decline after 1960 in the central city share of total SMSA manufacturing jobs, shown earlier in Figure 6-2, is further exemplified here. Whereas total manufacturing jobs increased by 7 percent, the central city lost 20 percent and the suburbs gained 56 percent. That is, the city lost close to 6,000 jobs while the suburbs gained close to 9,000. Less dramatic, but still quite substantial, similar shifts occurred in the other industries. The net result was to reduce the central city's share of all SMSA jobs from 70 percent in 1960 to 61 percent in 1967.

Underlying Dynamics

The development of the New Haven SMSA and the growth of its employment are, of course, closely tied to what happens in other parts of the nation. New

---

[c]In the remainder of this chapter we shall mostly deal with the 1960-67 period because the data available for those years is particularly rich.

Table 6-1
Jobs in the U.S. and in the New Haven SMSA, 1960 and 1967

Industry	*U.S.*					*New Haven SMSA*				
	1960		*1967*		*Percent Change: 1960-1967*	*1960*		*1967*		*Percent Change 1960-1967*
	No. (000)	*%*	*No. (000)*	*%*	*%*	*No.*	*%*	*No.*	*%*	*%*
(1)	(2)	(3)	(4)	(5)	(6)	(7)	(8)	(9)	(10)	(11)
Manufacturing	17,126	26.0	19,824	26.0	15.8	45,110	35.7	48,144	32.1	6.7
Construction, Transportation, Communication and Utilities	7,601	11.5	8,217	10.8	8.1	18,955	15.0	20,344	13.5	7.3
Trade	12,299	18.7	13,935	18.3	13.3	24,250	19.2	29,387	19.6	21.2
Finance, Insurance Real Estate, Services, Government	23,349	35.5	29,845	39.2	27.8	38,212	30.2	52,305	34.8	36.9
Agriculture, Mining	5,452	8.3	4,279	5.6	−21.5	0	0.0	0	0.0	0.0
Total	65,827	100.0	76,100	100.0	15.6	126,527	100.0	150,180	100.0	18.7

Source: Derived from Survey of Current Business [21], Connecticut Labor Department [4], and U.S. Bureau of the Census [19].

Table 6-2
1960 Jobs and 1960-1967 Growth Rates by Industry and City/Suburbs

	City		*Suburbs*		*SMSA*	
Industry	*1960 Jobs*	*1960-67 Growth %*	*1960 Jobs*	*1960-67 Growth %*	*1960 Jobs*	*1960-67 Growth %*
(1)	(2)	(3)	(4)	(5)	(6)	(7)
Manufacturing	29,159	−20.2	15,951	55.9	45,110	6.7
Construction, Transportation, Communication and Utilities	14,235	−1.2	4,720	33.1	18,955	7.3
Trade	15,190	8.7	9,060	42.2	24,250	21.2
Finance, Insurance, Real Estate, Services, Government	29,542	29.6	8,670	61.6	38,212	36.9
Total	88,126	4.5	38,401	51.2	126,527	18.7

Source: See Table 6-1.

Haven cannot be studied and understood in isolation—a point which has already been made several times. Ideally we would like to have a verified theory or model explaining and replicating the decision processes of businessmen and other administrators in all regions and industries. We would like to know more about what determines the flow of jobs (as well as people) between regions and what determines the nationwide decline of employment in some industries and growth in others. Unfortunately much remains to be done before a comprehensive and operational set of theories is available.[d] Meanwhile simple judgemental approaches have to be used. We have chosen to rely on available predictions of developments in the national economy which we use as a basis for our predictions for New Haven, assuming that the SMSA will continue to develop largely as it has in the recent past relative to the nation as a whole. Total employment growth up to 1980, and growth by industry were predicted for the twelve industries defined in Table 6-3. The number of jobs in agriculture and mining was very small and was neglected for the SMSA. The results are presented in Table 6-4.

[d] John R. Meyer has presented a good overview of the tasks ahead in the field of regional economics[10]. See also Perloff et al. [14] and Karaska and Bramhall [9].

Table 6-3
Industrial Categories in the New Haven Study

Industry No.		*SIC Code*[1]
1	Non-durable Manufacturing	20-23, 26-31
2	Durable Manufacturing	19, 24, 25, 32-39
3	Construction	15-17
4	Transportation	40-47
5	Communication and Utilities	48, 49
6	Wholesale Trade	50
7	Retail Trade	53-59
8	Finance, Insurance, and Real Estate	60-67
9	Services	70-89
10	Government	91-94
11	Agriculture	01-09
12	Mining	10-14

[1]As established by the Bureau of the Budget, Executive Office of the President, in 1957 and revised in 1967.

Total employment in New Haven increased at a slightly higher rate than national employment over the last decade, and this trend can be expected to continue because of the shift in New Haven's employment from slow- to fast-growing industries, as discussed earlier. A 2.0 percent annual growth rate has been assumed for New Haven between 1970 and 1980, as compared to an expected growth rate for the nation's employment of about 1.9 percent per year up to 1980.[e] This estimate for New Haven may be relatively conservative.

In predicting how the growth in total employment would be distributed over industries, we assumed that the number of manufacturing jobs would remain approximately constant—that is, the relative decline of manufacturing employment would continue—whereas jobs in finance, insurance, real estate, services, and government would increase substantially. Table 6-4 compares our prediction of the New Haven job structure in 1980 with the national structure in the same year, as predicted by the U.S. Bureau of Labor Statistics (after minor adjustments for definitional differences). Considering New Haven's history and its most recent development, we expect that by 1980 it will have a higher proportion of its employment in the non-manufacturing and non-agricultural industries than the nation as a whole—80 percent versus 73 percent—whereas the proportions were the same in 1967—68 percent.

Before examining where the new jobs will be located within the SMSA, let us take a look at the New Haven "labor market"—that is, the interaction between employers and job-seekers.

[e]See U.S. Bureau of Labor Statistics [20].

Table 6-4
Changes in the Job Structure for the U.S. and the New Haven SMSA, 1967-1980 (Percent)

	United States		*New Haven*	
Industry	*1967* *(1)*	*1980* *(2)*	*1967* *(3)*	*1980* *(4)*
Manufacturing	26.0	23.4	32.1	19.9
Construction, Transportation, Communication and Utilities	10.8	10.7	13.5	11.7
Trade	18.3	18.4	19.6	21.0
Finance, Insurance, Real Estate, Services, Government	39.2	44.0	34.8	47.4
Agriculture, Mining	5.6	3.5	0.0	0.0
Total	100.0	100.0	100.0	100.0

Source: See Table 6-1.

The New Haven Labor Market

Earlier we mentioned that the rates of in- and out-migration from the SMSA vary with the relative performance of the New Haven economy vis-a-vis the national one. The measure of relative performance which we found most useful in explaining the variation in migration rates was the ratio between the local and national unemployment rates.[f] For instance, when this ratio is higher than one, i.e., when the New Haven unemployment rate is higher than the national one, there is a decline in the normal rate of in-migration and an increase in the normal rate of out-migration. The opposite is true when the ratio is less than one, as discussed in detail in Chapter 4. This means that the growth rate of metropolitan jobs is a major determinant of the growth of the SMSA. By changing the predicted job growth we also change the population growth. This one-way causation is consistent with our findings about the past development of New Haven, and there is no reason to expect that the future will be different. For certain other parts of the U.S. this theory is less likely to be true, particularly for areas that attract a large number of retired people who are not sensitive to employment opportunities. The fact that total employment growth is an important factor in our predictions of the total growth of New Haven is one of the reasons why, in a later chapter, we shall experiment with alternative job growth rates.

[f]The unemployment rate is defined as the ratio, expressed in percent, between the number of people without a job and looking for one (the unemployed) and the sum of working and unemployed persons (the labor force).

The importance of the labor market segment of our model should be obvious by now. It links the growth-determining job segment with the population and household segment discussed in Chapter 4. The central elements of this link are the unemployment rates by type of person. These rates can be derived from a knowledge of the number of jobs in each industry, the occupational structure of jobs in each industry, and the likely occupation of each type of person. The mechanics for doing this are a little complicated and will not be dealt with in detail here.[g] In a nutshell, though, occupation serves as the common denominator. People and jobs are broken down by occupation. Knowing the odds that each type of person will be in the labor force and knowing the number of persons and jobs in each occupational category, one can make an estimate of the supply of and demand for workers of each occupation. The balance of supply and demand determines the unemployment rates.[h]

The results of this analysis for 1960 are presented in Table 6-5. Once

Table 6-5
Labor Force, Jobs, and Unemployment Rates by Occupation for the New Haven SMSA, 1960

Occupation (1)	*Labor Force (2)*	*Jobs (3)*	*Unemployment Rate % (4)*
Professional, technical and kindred	18,590	18,307	1.5
Managers and Proprietors	11,837	11,594	2.0
Clerical and kindred	23,713	22,921	3.3
Sales	10,107	9,681	4.2
Craftsmen, Foremen, and kindred	20,010	19,103	4.5
Operatives and kindred	29,499	27,748	5.9
Service Workers	13,253	12,441	6.1
Laborers	5,347	4,732	11.5
Total	132,356	126,527	4.4

Sources: Derived from U.S. Bureau of the Census [16, 17, 19] and Connecticut Labor Department [4].

[g]For a detailed description of how this is done, see Birch, Atkinson, Sandström, and Stack [1], Sections III and VIII.

[h]In our analysis we made a distinction between available and filled jobs—a distinction which we need not discuss in detail here. It was assumed that a certain proportion of available jobs would be unfilled because of friction in the labor market and that this proportion would increase with a declining unemployment rate. The least friction was assumed in the

unemployment by occupation has been determined, it is possible to work backwards through the procedure just described and estimate unemployment by type of person and by industry.

One key to estimating unemployment rates is knowing who is, or would like to be, in the labor force—the so-called "labor force participation rate." The participation rate can be expressed as the proportion of persons of each type working or seeking work. Table 6-6 presents the participation rates found in the New Haven SMSA in 1960. The rates vary with the age of the person, being highest in the 40 to 64 age group. They also vary with education; in the 20 to 39 age group persons with high school education have a lower participation rate than those with less or more education, for instance. We also notice that people with high education tend to remain in the labor force longer than people with less education. The reason for the very low participation rates for persons 0 to 19 years old with less than high school education is, of course, that most of them are less than 17 years old and are still going to school.

In our study we have assumed that the participation rates are constant over time for each type of person. As the composition of the population changes, the overall rate will change, however. For instance, with the minority population constituting a successively larger proportion of the total population, the overall participation rate will increase because the participation rates of minority persons are higher than those of native- and foreign-born persons. In fact, the overall rate for the SMSA increased slightly from 1960 to 1970 according to the Census, from about 43 percent to about 44 percent.

The Location of Jobs Within the SMSA

Proceeding from the national and regional levels, we shall now consider the decision processes through which employers determine the location of their plants and businesses within the SMSA. In so doing we shall distinguish between manufacturing and non-manufacturing jobs, paying more attention to the former than to the latter. For one thing, much more data was available on manufacturing jobs and their changing location than on other kinds of jobs. Also, comparatively little is known about what determines the intrametropolitan location of manufacturing jobs, and substantial controversy surrounds what little is known. Finally, the location of manufacturing jobs in New Haven is rapidly shifting from the city to the suburbs with wide-ranging consequences for the spatial pattern of the SMSA. The causes of this rapid shift must be better understood than at the present if one wants to make even short-term predictions of the area's spatial development.

---

professional and managerial occupations and the most in the low-skill service and laborer occupations.

Table 6-6
Labor Force Participation Rates in the New Haven SMSA by Type of Person in 1960

		Native			*Foreign-Born*			*Minority*		
		<HS	*HS*	*>HS*	*<HS*	*HS*	*>HS*	*<HS*	*HS*	*>HS*
Age	0-19	.048	.616	.365	.071	.712	.634	.048	.748	.997
	20-39	.677	.594	.666	.661	.599	.708	.688	.655	.778
	40-64	.702	.681	.698	.699	.713	.806	.740	.748	.872
	65+	.178	.235	.222	.183	.216	.425	.218	.258	.277

Source: U.S. Bureau of the Census [16, 19].

The location of manufacturing jobs was studied on an establishment, or plant basis—that is, we studied individual plants, with known employment sizes, rather than the jobs per se. In our study of non-manufacturing jobs, we used a more aggregate approach, disregarding the fact that jobs are grouped into establishments of various sizes. No comprehensive data on non-manufacturing establishments by size and location were available. The size variation is relatively small among non-manufacturing establishments, however, and the average size also is small. The neglect of behavioral differences among business managers in each of the non-manufacturing industries should thus not seriously affect our results.

Manufacturing Jobs. We shall begin by analyzing the life cycle of manufacturing plants—what might be called corporate demography. Six types of manufacturing plants were defined along two dimensions: employment size and type of product.[i] In Table 6-7 the number of plants of each type in 1959 and 1967 is presented, by location. While there was an overall increase of 39 plants over the eight years, the city lost 96 plants and the suburbs gained 135 plants. This is a remarkable shift over such a short time period. The ways in which it happened are what we shall try to describe and explain.

The life cycle and the changing location of plants were studied in terms of five processes: (1) the foundation of a new plant or the movement of a plant into the SMSA from another part of the country, both of which we shall call a "birth" of a new plant, (2) movement within the SMSA, (3) the closing or shutdown of a plant or the movement of one out of the SMSA, a "death",

[i]Three employment sizes—small (1-9 employees), medium-sized (10-249 employees), and large (250 employees or more)—and two types of product—durable and non-durable manufacturing were used. The average employment sizes in the three groups were about 3, 49, and 743 employees, respectively.

Table 6-7
Number of Manufacturing Plants in the New Haven SMSA in 1959 and 1967 by Type and by City and Suburbs

		Non-Durable Manufacturing			*Durable Manufacturing*			
Employment Size:		*1-9*	*10-249*	*250+*	*1-9*	*10-249*	*250+*	*Total*
Type:		1	2	3	4	5	6	
1959	City	116	151	10	121	79	14	491
	Suburbs	54	49	2	105	101	8	319
	SMSA	170	200	12	226	180	22	810
1967	City	99	123	10	81	68	14	395
	Suburbs	73	81	4	136	150	10	454
	SMSA	172	204	14	217	218	24	849

Source: Our basic data source was the directories of manufacturing establishments published by the Connecticut Labor Department [3], which included the name, the address, the employment size, the 2-digit SIC (Standard Industrial Classification) code, and the major products of each plant located in the SMSA. The addresses of individual plants were matched with a special reference tape for the SMSA which contained the census tract number for each street address (the procedure is more fully described in ADMATCH [15]. About 70 percent of the establishments could be assigned to census tracts using this technique. In the remaining cases either the addresses of the establishments or the reference tape was incomplete and maps and additional data sources (including directories published by the Greater New Haven Chamber of Commerce [6]) were used to determine the location of the establishments. Special care had to be taken to reveal name changes to avoid exaggerating the number of "births" and "deaths" of manufacturing plants.

(4) expansion, and (5) contraction The degree to which each of these five processes affected the size and location of plants between 1959 and 1967 is quite impressive.

Table 6-8 shows the three components of change which led to the net increase of 39 in the total number of plants, and which also resulted in the overall shift from the city to the suburbs. There were 39 more births than deaths (306 births versus 267 deaths) causing the increase in the total number of plants. The shift from the city to the suburbs was composed of a net outmovement of 47 plants from the city to the suburbs and an excess of 49 deaths over births in the city. That is, about 50 percent of the city's loss of 96 plants was caused by moves to the suburbs and 50 percent by an excess of deaths over births.

Table 6-7 revealed a substantial increase in medium-sized plants, with 10-49 employees. In Table 6-9 we can see what the components of the increase were: (1) a substantial excess of births over deaths among small plants coupled with (2) a net expansion of small plants into larger ones. Here a pattern begins to emerge to which we shall return shortly: small plants experience a rapid

Table 6-8
Components of Overall Change in the Number of Manufacturing Plants in the New Haven SMSA, 1959 to 1967, by City and Suburbs

	New Haven City (1)	*Suburbs* (2)	*SMSA Total* (3)
Births	121	185	306
Deaths	−170	− 97	−267
Net Intrametropolitan Moves	− 47	47	0
Total Change	− 96	135	39
Number of Plants in 1959	491	319	810
Number of Plants in 1967	395	454	849

Source: See Table 6-7

Table 6-9
Components of the Changing Size Distribution of Manufacturing Plants in the New Haven SMSA, 1959 to 1967

	Employment Size			
	1-9 (1)	*10-249* (2)	*250+* (3)	*Total*
Expansion and Contraction (net)	− 47	41	6	0
Births	190	114	2	306
Deaths	−150	−113	−4	−267
Total Change	− 7	42	4	39

Source: See Table 6-7.

turnover, the successful and well managed ones expanding into larger sizes where they age and die.

Finally, to complete this overview, Table 6-10 shows gross expansion and contraction between 1959 and 1967. Despite our relatively broad size categories, there were still 80 plants which changed size. The net expansion of 47 plants from the smallest to larger sizes, observed in Table 6-9, was composed of 58 expanding plants and 11 contracting ones. One plant jumped from the smallest to the largest size category.

By now the rather straightforward picture presented earlier—showing a net increase of 39 manufacturing plants in the SMSA—has become quite complex.

Table 6-10
Expansion and Contraction of Manufacturing Plants in the New Haven SMSA, 1959 to 1967

	To Employment Size			
From Employment Size	*1-9*	*10-249*	*250+*	*Total From*
(1)	(2)	(3)	(4)	(5)
1-9	–	57	1	58
10-249	11	–	8	19
250+	0	3	–	3
Total To	11	60	9	80

Source: See Table 6-7.

The underlying processes–births, deaths, expansion, and contraction–are highly dynamic. It is obvious that the key to an understanding of how the manufacturers locate lies in an analysis of these processes.

Figure 6-3 summarizes our discussion so far. It shows the number of births, deaths, expansions and contractions between 1959 and 1967, by employment size of the plants. One can see how the group of small plants functions as a "testbed"–many come and go; a small number survive the test and expand into the next larger size group. Similarly, there is a significant amount of net expansion from medium-sized to large plants. A balance is maintained through an excess of births over deaths among small plants and vice versa among large plants. Successful manufacturing plants tend to be born small and die large. Some of them slowly reduce their employment before they transpire. The choice of location for a new, small plant is thus extremely important. It often remains at its first location throughout its life, even if the site is unsuitable for the larger size to which it may expand. There are many examples of old and large plants in New Haven city that chose their present location when they started as small plants, but which now would prefer a suburban location. More often than not, a move is not a financially viable alternative for these old plants, which in many cases face a dwindling market for their products. The city has trapped them in the later stages of their life cycle.

The Location of New Plants. The managers of the plants born between 1959 and 1967–the new plants–showed a strong preference for suburban locations, as Table 6-11 indicates. Over 60 percent of them chose the suburbs over the city. But in 1959 only 39 percent of all plants were located in the suburbs, a percentage which by 1967 had increased to 53 percent, still far from 60 percent. The explanation for this difference is simple and obvious. The location of plants in 1959 did not reflect the actual preferences and needs of their owners at that

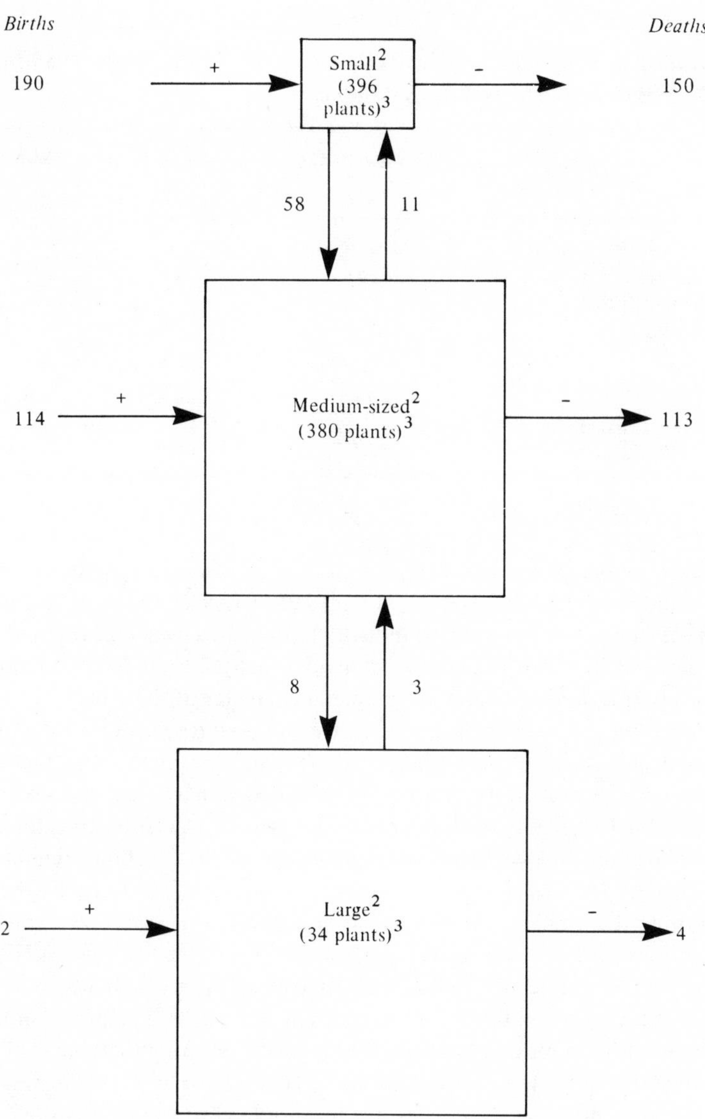

Source: See Table 6-7

[1]The area of each square is proportional to the total number of employees in plants of the corresponding size in 1959.

[2]Number of plants is as of 1959.

[3]Small: 1-9 employees; Medium-sized: 10-249 employees; Large: 250 employees or more.

Figure 6-3 Births, Deaths, Expansion and Contraction of Manufacturing Plants in the New Haven SMSA, 1959 to 1967[1]

Table 6-11
The Location of Manufacturing Plants in 1959 and of New Plants, 1959 to 1967, in the New Haven SMSA, by City and Suburbs

	New Haven City (1)	*Suburbs* (2)	*SMSA Total* (3)
Absolute Numbers:			
1959 Plants	491	319	810
New Plants (Births) 1959-1967	121	185	306
Percentages:			
1959 Plants	60.6%	39.4%	100.0%
New Plants (Births) 1959-1967	39.5%	60.5%	100.0%

Source: See Table 6-7.

time. Most of the plants had been set up several decades ago. In a floor-area survey conducted in New Haven city in 1961, it was found that about 70 percent of the city's commercial-industrial floor area was constructed before 1930. Since then there have been dramatic changes both in production and transportation technologies and in the spatial character of the city.

The simplest and best indicator of actual site preferences of manufacturers is the chosen location of new plants. If we can determine what factors are considered in the evaluation of a potential site for a new plant and the way in which the final choice is arrived at, we are then in a position to estimate the preferred location of establishments. Knowledge of the location preferences of new plants is also useful when it comes to understanding decisions regarding intrametropolitan moves, deaths, expansion and contraction. By comparing preferred locations with the actual one, as we did in Table 6-11, we can obtain a measure of the degree of "imbalance" that exists—a measure which we have found to be a good indicator of the extent to which a manufacturer feels dissatisfied with his present location. For instance, referring to Table 6-11 again, a manufacturer who was located in the city in the early 1960's was in all likelihood very dissatisfied and was much more likely to move than one of his colleagues in the suburbs.

In the past, two approaches have been used in the study of location preferences of manufacturers. In one approach, the purely statistical one, the variation in the number of jobs with factors such as the distance from the center of the city is analyzed. In another approach, the behavioral one, attempts are made to understand the decision process of manufacturers—to find out what they look for and how they evaluate what they find. It is this latter approach we have followed.

One earlier behavioral study of manufacturers deserves special mention: Hoover and Vernon's *Anatomy of a Metropolis*[j] and related publications, where a wealth of interesting and well-developed findings are presented. Hoover and Vernon found that four factors have a dominant influence on manufacturers: space, transportation, labor, and external economies. Present production technology requiring single-story plant layouts, and the need for expansion space, result in a preference for suburban location. Developments in transportation, "from river to rail to rubber," have made firms less dependent on natural characteristics, more foot-loose. Intrametropolitan differences in labor costs and varying accessibility to a labor force also affect a manufacturer's choice of location.[k]

Hoover and Vernon also point out that small manufacturing plants usually depend to a large extent on services and facilities provided by others. Small plants may, for instance, share buildings, or make use of outside accountants, and are often heavily dependent on the services of wholesalers. Larger plants are able to "internalize" many more functions than small plants are, and as a consequence they are much freer in their choice of location. The central city has traditionally been the place where small-scale manufacturers must go to find these services, and, as expected, one normally finds a higher concentration of small than of large plants in the central city of a metropolitan region. This was the case in the New York region as Hoover and Vernon point out.[l] As a result of this tendency, the central city has been thought of as a spawning ground, or incubator, for manufacturing plants–it is where they are born in an environment that fits their needs. The successful ones supposedly expand and, in the process, internalize many of the functions which, for a small plant, must be purchased from the outside. Finally, they may move out to the suburbs.

In New Haven, we found that this central city incubator phenomenon does not explain recent behavior very well. Between 1959 and 1967, for example, the suburban share (61 percent) of new, small plants was significantly greater than the central city share (39 percent). Furthermore, the odds that a new plant will locate in the central city was not a strong function of size. Plants with more than 10 employees were just as likely to select the central city as plants employing nine or less. Evidently, the economies of the suburbs are now so developed and varied that the shared facilities and services required by small manufacturers can be found there. Small firms no longer have to spend their first few years in the

---

[j]See Hoover and Vernon [8].

[k]Similarly, it was found in a recent study of Boston's manufacturers [2] that space and labor were dominating among the factors which they considered. For instance, the majority of the Boston firms that at the end of 1969 were planning to relocate cited the need for expansion space and one-story layout as the most compelling reasons for a move. Better proximity to skilled and unskilled labor was the second most important reason.

[l]Hoover and Vernon [8], pp. 45-46.

central city. The implications are wide-ranging. Not only does this mean that the city in the future will attract fewer small plants, but it will also, in the long run, have fewer large plants. Many of the small plants that, in the past, were successfully reared in the city, never left for the suburbs. In many instances they became trapped, as we discussed earlier. By the time they realized that a suburban location would be much more suitable, they had already invested too much in their present location or their future no longer looked bright enough to make a move financially viable. In the future, plants such as these will be "trapped" in the suburbs.

With the exception of the central city incubator notion, our findings with respect to New Haven manufacturers were quite similar to those of Hoover and Vernon in New York. Space and labor are two factors that have a definite influence on locational choices, whereas natural physical characteristics—such as the harbor and the rivers—are losing importance. The remainder of this section looks more closely at the specific factors which we studied and the ways in which the managers of new plants evaluated them.

There are three factors to which the managers of both small and large new plants in New Haven pay particular attention when they evaluate potential locations: the job and traffic congestion in the area, proximity to labor force, and the number of plants of the same size already located in the area (the clustering factor). The first factor—quantified in the form of a "congestion index"[m]—is a good composite indicator of space availability and the ease with which goods can be transported to and from the area. The more congested the area is, the less attractive it is to manufacturers, all other things being equal. A high employment density in a district will lead to a high congestion index. And even if the employment density in a certain district is low, the index for the district may still be high if there are many jobs in neighboring districts and if the transportation system is such that the driving time from these districts to the one in question is short. In such a case, we can generally expect much of the traffic generated in neighboring districts to pass through the district, and this traffic clearly reduces its attractiveness from the point of view of a manufacturer. Large establishments were found to be much more sensitive to this index than smaller ones.

The proximity of a potential site to the labor force affects its suitability for a plant.[n] The more accessible to the labor force the area is, the more attractive it is as a location for a manufacturing plant. As expected, large plants are much more sensitive to labor force proximity than small plants are. The absolute level

---

[m]The congestion index is estimated for each district as the weighted sum of all jobs in this and all other districts, the weights being the inverse of the driving time from the district where the jobs are located to the district for which we are computing the index.

[n]The proximity index is estimated as the weighted sum of the labor force over districts of residence, the weights being the inverse of the driving time from the district of residence to the district being evaluated.

of sensitivity is not very high in New Haven, however, because of the short driving times involved, as discussed previously.

The third factor which we studied and quantified was the attention which manufacturers pay to the number of plants of the same size already located in an area. To a large extent this factor measures the availability in the area of certain facilities and services which plants of each size require—the more plants of the same size there are in the area, the more attractive it is, all other things being equal. Large plants were found to be less dependent on this factor than small plants are, as one would expect.

The three above mentioned factors—congestion, labor proximity, and clustering—are considered by the managers of both small and large plants. Small plants were also found to be affected by two additional factors: the number of large plants in an area and the number of jobs in wholesale trade. The more large plants there are, the less attractive an area is to small plants. This fact seems to be related to what we might call "external diseconomies." Large plants tend to require external facilities and services of a scale that are not suited to the needs of small plants. Small plants appear unwilling to pay a premium for these facilities and services and tend, therefore, to gravitate towards areas where the general scale of operations is relatively small.

The importance to small plants of being located close to wholesale trade firms is an example of the strong need these plants have for externally provided services. Wholesalers often handle many important functions for small manufacturing plants, including much of the paper work involved in shipping both raw materials and products—functions which larger plants can internalize.

The five factors discussed above explain some 90 percent of the location choices made by managers of new manufacturing plants in New Haven between 1959 and 1967. The factors are used to assess the odds that each type of new plant will select each of the 23 districts. These odds are called 'attractiveness scores." A comparison of (1) the odds that a new plant of a certain type will select a district, with (2) the number of existing plants of the same type already there yields our "imbalance" measure. A district that presently contains many manufacturing plants, but that no new plant would select as a location, is way "out of balance." Many of the managers now located in the district are, in all likelihood, unhappy with their surroundings. In the following sections we shall see how the attractiveness scores and the imbalance concept can be used to predict the origin and destination of movers, as well as the location of deaths, expansions, and contractions.

Movers. An intrametropolitan mover makes two important decisions: he decides to leave his present location, and he decides on a new location. The propensity to move (or mobility rate), was more than three times higher in the central city than in the suburbs between 1959 and 1967, as Table 6-12 shows. This variation is proportional to the degree of imbalance between the preferred and the actual

Table 6-12
The Location of Manufacturing Plants in 1959 and of New Plants, 1959 to 1967, and the Number of Moving Plants, 1959 to 1967, in the New Haven SMSA, by City and Suburbs

	New Haven City (1)	*Suburbs* (2)	*SMSA Total* (3)
Absolute Numbers:			
1959 Plants	491	319	810
New Plants (Births) 1959-1967	121	185	306
Moving Plants 1959-1967	119	24	143
Percentages:			
1959 Plants	60.6%	39.4%	100.0%
New Plants (Births) 1959-1967	39.5%	60.5%	100.0%
Moving Plants 1959-1967, Relative to 1959 Plants (Mobility Rates)	24.2%	7.5%	17.7%

Source: See Table 6-7.

location of manufacturing plants. The very high mobility rate in the city is caused by the dissatisfaction experienced by manufacturers located there.[o]

The mobility rate also varies with the size of the plants, being slightly higher for small than for medium-sized and large ones. More interesting is the finding that the mobility rates of medium-sized and large plants are about twice as sensitive to imbalances in the location of plants as are the mobility rates of small plants. That is, the managers of larger plants seem to be much more sensitive to the suitability of their present location than do owners of small plants. This may be a reflection both of a higher degree of flexibility and adaptability on the part of managers of small plants, and a higher awareness of the optimum operating conditions on the part of owners of larger plants.

[o]A similar but less comprehensive analysis of the changing spatial distribution of manufacturing establishments has been done by Moses and Williamson for Chicago over the period of 1950 to 1964 [11]. Their data covered only a sample of intrametropolitan moves and did not include births and deaths. They did a regression analysis where the number of origins (leavers) was the dependent variable and the number of firms and the distance from the center were chosen as independent variables. Their conclusion was that the propensity to move was fairly constant over the entire metropolitan area and that therefore the changing spatial distribution must be caused by the distribution of the destinations of the movers. They assumed that the number of births and deaths was insignificant relative to the number of movers. This was not the case in New Haven. First, the propensity to move was about three times higher in the city than in the suburbs, 24 percent versus 8 percent. Second, together births and deaths caused a slightly larger change in the spatial distribution than movers did.

Table 6-13
The Location of Manufacturing Plants in 1959 and of New Plants, 1959 to 1967, and the Destinations of Moving Plants, 1959 to 1967, in the New Haven SMSA, by City and Suburbs

	New Haven City (1)	*Suburbs* (2)	*SMSA Total* (3)
Absolute Numbers:			
1959 Plants	491	319	810
New Plants (Births) 1959-1967	121	185	306
Destinations of Moving Plants 1959-1967	72	71	143
Percentages:			
1959 Plants	60.6%	39.4%	100.0%
New Plants (Births) 1959-1967	39.5%	60.5%	100.0%
Destinations of Moving Plants 1959-1967	50.3%	49.7%	100.0%

Source: See Table 6-7.

The decisions made by movers on where to settle down reveal one very interesting thing, as indicated in Table 6-13. They tend to prefer the city to a greater extent than new manufacturers do. Whereas only 40 percent of all new plants were located in the city, 50 percent of the movers chose a location there. Most of the movers came from the central city, as we have seen, and it is obvious that they tended to move relatively short distances.

The different ways in which moving and new manfacturers perceive the suitability of particular sites for the location of their plants can best be explained by the assumption that there are intrametropolitan relocation costs that increase with the distance moved, and which are of such a magnitude as to affect the choice of a new location. Such relocation costs consist mainly of the attenuation and breaking of ties with customers and suppliers of raw materials and services. As most of the movers came from the central city, the existence of distance-dependent relocation costs would tend to increase the number of arrivers in or close to the city relative to what it would be if there were no such costs.[p]

It was also found that many movers tended to limit their consideration of alternative sites to areas with which they were relatively familiar, and that the degree of their familiarity decreased with the distance from their original site, with the distance measured in accessibility terms, i.e., driving time. The effects

[p]Moses and Williamson observed a similar pattern for Chicago manufacturers [11], p. 216.

of this limited-information-and-consideration factor and the existence of distance-varying relocation costs are similar (and to some extent the root causes of these factors overlap).

A third reason why movers tend to prefer the city lies in the fact that many of them operate in declining industries in which their future may not appear very bright. They look, therefore, for relatively inexpensive and short term rental space. Such space is still more commonly available in the city than in the suburbs. Incidentally, this leads to a relatively high turnover in certain industries and in certain parts of the city—with some plants constantly looking for short-term and cheap space—and contributes to the higher mobility rates observed in the city.

Except for the three factors just discussed, movers appear to evaluate potential locations in much the same way as new manufacturers do. The attractiveness scores of various districts from the point of view of a mover can be determined, therefore, by reducing the attractiveness scores for new plants by a factor proportional to the driving time from the mover's district of origin to the district being evaluated.

Table 6-14 summarizes the moving experience of the New Haven plants between 1959 and 1967, showing both origins and destinations. There was not a single move from the suburbs to the city over the eight years, while there were 47 moves the other way. The amount of internal mobility within the city was quite high—72 moves.

Deaths. The variation in death rates between the city and the suburbs (Table 6-15) follows the same pattern as the variation in mobility rates. Managers in the city, however, were only slightly more sensitive to spatial imbalances in the location of plants than were managers in the suburbs—the death rate in the city was 35 percent, versus 30 percent in the suburbs. This should be compared with the much larger difference in mobility rates between the city and the suburbs observed earlier—24 percent versus 8 percent. The death of a plant is often related to financial and other deep-rooted difficulties which are not directly tied

Table 6-14
Intrametropolitan Moves of Manufacturing Plants in the New Haven SMSA, 1959 to 1967

From	*City*	*Suburbs*	*Total From*
City	72	47	119
Suburbs	0	24	24
Total To	72	71	143

Source: See Table 6-7.

Table 6-15
The Location of Manufacturing Plants in 1959 and of New Plants, 1959 to 1967, and the Number of Closed Plants, 1959 to 1967, in the New Haven SMSA, by City and Suburbs

	New Haven City (1)	*Suburbs* (2)	*SMSA Total* (3)
Absolute Numbers:			
1959 Plants	491	319	810
New Plants (Births) 1959-1967	121	185	306
Closed Plants (Deaths) 1959-1967	170	97	267
Percentages:			
1959 Plants	60.6%	39.4%	100.0%
New Plants (Births) 1959-1967	39.5%	60.5%	100.0%
Closed Plants (Deaths) 1959-1967 Relative to Plants in 1959 (Death Rates)	34.6%	30.4%	33.0%

Source: See Table 6-7.

to the suitability of the plant's present location. A move to a more suitable location would probably be too late to save the plant at a stage when its closing is being considered. Plants that are strongly negatively affected by their location choose to move rather than to die, explaining in part the much higher sensitivity of mobility rates than of death rates to spatial imbalances. The death rates decrease with the size of the plant. The death rate of large plants is slightly more sensitive to spatial imbalances than is the death rate of small plants.

Expansion and Contraction. The propensity of managers to reduce the size of their plants varies relatively little with spatial imbalances. As in the case of death rates, contraction is apparently tied to the life cycle of the plant and to more deep-rooted difficulties than to dissatisfaction with the present location.

The propensity to expand is slightly more sensitive to dissatisfaction with location. Managers of medium-sized plants appear to pay more attention to spatial imbalances in making their expansion decisions than do managers of small plants. The expansion rate of small plants is fairly constant over the entire SMSA, whereas the expansion rate of medium-sized plants is smaller in the city than in the suburbs.

Summary. We have seen that the five demographic processes of manufacturing plants—births, movements, deaths, expansion and contraction—must be properly understood and incorporated into a theory of manufacturing location in order to fully explain the changing location of manufacturing jobs. The locational decisions made by the managers of new plants indicate the basic attractiveness, or desirability of various parts of the SMSA. Existing plants cannot adjust their location to the requirements of changing production technologies and changing spatial conditions without a time lag. There is thus always an imbalance between the actual location of plants and the preferred location. Mobility rates, death rates, contraction and expansion rates vary in proportion to the imbalance. Movers were found to evaluate potential destination sites the same way new manufacturers do, but with one important difference: movers tend to consider relocation costs which increase with the distance moved, with the result that they prefer sites close to their original locations to a larger extent than new manufacturers do.

Non-Manufacturing Jobs. The approach we follow in our analysis and in making our projections for non-manufacturing jobs is quite similar to the one just outlined for manufacturing plants, with the major exception that we look at jobs directly rather than at firms or establishments. A set of attractiveness scores is determined for each industry, indicating what the preferred location pattern of jobs is. The existing pattern is then compared with the preferred one in order to identify any imbalances. It is assumed that imbalances will be reduced each year—through relocation of businesses, births, deaths, expansion, and contraction. Retailers are assumed to adjust very quickly to any imbalances, whereas businesses in transportation, communication and utilities, and government require up to a decade or more to adjust. The preferred location pattern is constantly changing, however, and as a result all industries will always experience a certain imbalance. This imbalance will, in general, be greater the lower the rate of adjustment of the industry.

Any increases in total employment in the SMSA are assumed to be located according to the attractiveness scores—that is, according to the preferred location pattern. The location of decreases in total employment is determined by existing imbalances—the larger the imbalance in an area, the more likely the area is to lose jobs.

Construction. Harris suggests that the location of construction jobs is related to "changes which are occurring in total employment and residential population by small area—since these imply new construction for possible establishments, residences, and public facilities."[q] In addition to these two factors—changes in the densities of employment and population—the absolute levels of employment and population were found to affect the number of construction jobs located in a particular area, mainly because of the need for maintenance and repair work.

[q]See Harris [7], p. 404.

Transportation. Historically the location of transportation jobs has been rather fixed, partly because of the fixed locations of rivers, natural harbors, and so forth, and partly because of the huge relocation costs for such facilities as railways. Trucks and a network of roads and highways have changed this to some extent, but there are still substantial discrepancies between the actual and preferred locations of transportation jobs.

We found that businessmen in the transportation industry prefer to be in close proximity to non-durable manufacturing plants, because of the demand for speedy transportation generated by this industry. Similarly, districts which are close to employment centers are, in general, attractive because of the generated demand for transportation. At the same time districts with high employment density themselves are less attractive, because of traffic congestion. Transportation managers prefer a low-density area with little traffic surrounded by areas with high employment density. They shun areas with high population density, mainly because of the expected unwillingness of residents to accept noisy, nighttime traffic in their neighborhood.

Communication and Utilities. This group is extremely diverse and difficult to analyze without further disaggregation. Nevertheless, it appears as though accessibility to the residential population is of importance, viewing the population as both customers and workers. High densities of transportation and retail jobs are less desirable because of the traffic-generating effect of these jobs.

Wholesale Trade. Wholesalers are attracted to districts that are close to employment centers in the same way that businessmen in the transportation industry are and for similar reasons. They also avoid, and are kept out of, areas with large numbers of high-income residents. Wholesaling is less of a nuisance industry, in terms of noise and safety, than transportation. It is therefore more acceptable to residents and is more likely to be found in a low-income area.

Retail Trade. The location of retail jobs is fairly sensitive to shifts in the location of the population. Retailers, though, are not so much interested in population density per se as they are in the accessibility of an area to the residential population. An accessibility index–similar to the one we discussed earlier for the proximity of a district for the labor force–was found to be a good measure of the effect.

People do much of their shopping in connection with their work–during lunch hours primarily. Total employment density was consequently found to be one of the factors retailers consider. In addition, retailers pay particular attention to the number of retail jobs already located in an area. They want to be located in close proximity to other retail stores–the clustering effect. Shoppers tend to prefer places where they can find a variety of retail stores within walking distance.

A high density of durable manufacturing jobs will reduce the attractiveness of an area to retailers. Durable manufacturing has some negative side-effects—such as noise, heavy truck traffic, air pollution, and so forth—which are likely to repel potential customers. Retailers seem to be fairly neutral to the presence of non-durable manufacturing, however. This is partly because the side-effects of this industry are less of a nuisance, and partly because there often is a local supplier-customer relationship between non-durable manufacturing and retailing.

Finance, Insurance, Real Estate, Services, and Government. Businessmen and administrators in these industries have locational preferences similar to those of retailers, with two exceptions: little attention is paid to the residential location of population, and the presence of non-durable, as well as durable manufacturing reduces an area's attractiveness. Apparently, jobs in these five industries are very attracted to areas with high employment densities. The clustering effect is strong.

A Note on Accuracy

At this point, a natural question is: How well can the many partial theories discussed in this chapter replicate the behavior of manufacturers and other businessmen when integrated with our assumptions about the behavior of private individuals, households, builders, discussed in the two preceding chapters? Table 6-16 presents the average percent errors which were observed when the simulation model incorporating all our assumptions was run from 1960 to 1967. The average percent error was about 18 percent at the finest level of detail at which we could check accuracy.

In evaluating the errors produced by the model, one must keep in mind the weaknesses of job data at the small area level. The starting data for 1960, as well as the test data for 1967, had to be pieced together from many different sources and adjusted to ensure consistency with the population, labor force, and employment data provided by the Census.[r] The accuracy of the job data is therefore substantially less than the accuracy of the population and household data. Our estimates of the job-data accuracy are also presented in Table 6-16. It appears that our simulated results are roughly comparable to the measurement accuracy of the data.

Summary and Conclusions

Our historical analysis of New Haven revealed a cyclical growth pattern,

---

[r]For the details of this derivation, see Birch, et al. [1].

Table 6-16
Average Percent Error for Jobs in 1967 for a 1960-1967 Run of the New Haven Model and Estimated Accuracy of the Data

Average Percent Error in 1967:

	Totals	*Marginals*
SMSA	0.1%	0.1%
District	6.2%	18.1%

Estimated Accuracy of the Data:

	Totals	*Marginals*
SMSA	±1%	± 5%
District	±7%	±15%

characterized by a growth period from about 1840 until just after World War I and a subsequent relative decline. There are indications, however, that a revival of New Haven is on its way. The area has a strong base in many tertiary industries and is rapidly increasing its employment in this sector.

The spatial analysis of New Haven reiterated and confirmed the decoupling phenomenon first mentioned in Chapter 2. The suburbs are becoming increasingly less dependent on the central city. In days gone by, small plants in need of supporting facilities had to locate in the city. Today they are as free in their choice between the city and the suburbs as the large plants are. The suburban economies are well enough developed to provide the same wide range of facilities and services as the city. The notion of the city as the primary incubator for manufacturing plants in the SMSA is no longer valid.

Time and again in this chapter we have observed the dependence of manufacturers and other businessmen and administrators on the location of people as well as other jobs. This dependence marks a shift from earlier days in New Haven when manufacturers largely determined the spatial development pattern of the SMSA. Eli Whitney and Oliver Winchester decided to locate their plants in Newhallville and just across the boundary in Hamden. First workers, and later entrepreneurs setting up retail and service businesses followed. Similar chains of events occurred elsewhere in the SMSA, all in conformity with a still prevailing theory of how urban spatial structure is determined: manufacturers select the locations of their plants largely independently of where households and other jobs are located; thereafter, first the households and then other businessmen follow in their footsteps. We have seen that the processes through which urban spatial patterns are determined are considerably more complex than this simple one-way causal chain of events. Workers simultaneously influence and react to the location of a new manufacturing facility.

References

1. Birch, Atkinson, Sandström and Stack. *The New Haven Laboratory.* Lexington, Mass.: Lexington Books, D.C. Heath & Co., 1974.

2. City of Boston, Economic Development and Industrial Commission. *Boston's Industry: A Profile based on a Survey of Manufacturers.* Boston, March 1970.

3. Connecticut Labor Department. *Directory of Connecticut Manufacturing and Mechanical Establishments.* Hartford, Connecticut: State of Connecticut, Various Years.

4. Connecticut Labor Department. *Employment by SIC Code in the New Haven Labor Market Area.* Unpublished Tabulations, Various Years.

5. Greater New Haven Chamber of Commerce. *Connecticut's South Central Region An Economic Profile and Industrial Directory.* New Haven, Conn., December, 1966.

6. Greater New Haven Chamber of Commerce. *1969-1970 Economic Profile and Industrial Directory of South Central Connecticut.* New Haven, Conn., January, 1969.

7. Harris, Britton. "Quantitative Models of Urban Development: Their Role in Metropolitan Policy-Making" in *Issues in Urban Economics.* H. Perloff and L. Wingo Jr., (Editors). Baltimore: Resources for the Future Inc., The Johns Hopkins Press, 1968, pp. 363-412.

8. Hoover, Edgar and Raymond Vernon. *Anatomy of a Metropolis: The Changing Distribution of People and Jobs Within the New York Metropolitan Region.* Cambridge, Mass.: Harvard University Press, 1959.

9. Karaska, Gerald J. and David Bramhall (Editors). *Locational Analysis in Manufacturing.* Cambridge, Mass.: MIT Press, 1969.

10. Meyer, John R. "Regional Economics: A Survey," *The American Economic Review.* March 1963, pp. 19-54.

11. Moses, Leon and Harold F. Williamson, Jr. "The Location of Economic Activity in Cities" in *Papers and Proceedings of the American Economic Association.* Vol. 57, No. 2. May 1967, pp. 211-222.

12. New Haven Community Renewal Program. *Commercial-Industrial Floor Area Block Summary and Average Rating.* Technical Paper No. 8, New Haven, Connecticut, 1964.

13. Osterweis, Rollin G. *Three Centuries of New Haven.* New Haven: Yale University Press, 1953.

14. Perloff, Harvey S., Edgar S. Dunn Jr., Eric E. Lampard, Richard F. Muth. *Regions, Resources, and Economic Growth.* Baltimore: Resources for the Future, Inc., The Johns Hopkins Press, 1960.

15. U.S. Bureau of the Census. *ADMATCH: Users Manual: Census Use Study.* Washington, D.C.: U.S. Government Printing Office, 1970.

16. U.S. Bureau of the Census. *A Public Use Sample of Basic Records from the 1960 Census: Description and Technical Documentation.* Washington, D.C.: U.S. Government Printing Office, 1971.

17. U.S. Bureau of the Census. *U.S. Census of Population: 1960, Detailed Characteristics, Connecticut.* Final Report PC(1)-8D, Washington, D.C.: U.S. Government Printing Office, 1962.

18. U.S. Bureau of the Census. *U.S. Census of Population: 1960, Selected Area Reports, Standard Metropolitan Statistical Areas.* Final Report PC(3)-1D, Washington, D.C.: U.S. Government Printing Office, 1963.

19. U.S. Bureau of the Census. *U.S. Censuses of Population and Housing: 1960, Census Tracts.* Final Report PHC(1)-102, Washington, D.C.: U.S. Government Printing Office, 1961.

20. U.S. Bureau of Labor Statistics. *Patterns of U.S. Economic Growth,* Bulletin No. 1672. Washington, D.C.: Government Printing Office, 1970.

21. U.S. Office of Business Economics. *Survey of Current Business.* U.S. Department of Commerce, monthly periodical. Washington, D.C., Government Printing Office (various issues).

7 Patterns for the Future

The last few chapters have described how various different kinds of urban people appear to behave under a variety of circumstances. Now we will see what happens when they interact in a regional context. For the purposes of this chapter, the reader need only understand a few basic principles about the structure of the overall model in which the interactions take place.[a] Simply stated, they are:

1. Each part of the model simulates the behavior of some group of people acting in some capacity. One part, for example, simulates the initial selection of neighborhoods through which households drive on Sunday afternoons when looking for a new house. Another part simulates the decision of a builder to lay a foundation for a single-family home in, say, northern Hamden.
2. Each part simulates behavior by looking at the "world" (as described by all the variables in the model) through the eyes and mind of a person, and by making decisions the way we feel such a person would in fact make decisions were he or she "real."
3. The result of each decision–such as the builder's decision to lay a foundation and build a house in northern Hamden–affects the decisions of anyone else who happens to care about how many houses are in northern Hamden–because it affects the "world" which such a person observes. Persons affected in this manner might include households looking in Hamden for a place to live, landlords setting rents in Hamden (and elsewhere), mortgage bankers making loans, other builders deciding whether or not to lay a foundation themselves, and perhaps a businessman deciding where to locate a new store. The number of these cross-relationships, or feedback loops as they are sometimes called, is virtually limitless, and is determined by who looks at what when they make a decision. Some of the stronger and more significant ones were indicated in Figure 3-1.
4. Although the cross-relationships are many, they are frequently not direct. The parts are not bolted together the way they are in an aircraft. They relate indirectly the same way they in fact relate in the "real world." Families seeking new houses do not automatically buy the new one in northern Hamden simply because the builder built it. They look around in a number of

[a]The technically inclined reader is reminded that in Appendix B we give a brief overview of how the pieces relate, and that a far more detailed description is provided in Birch, Atkinson, Sandström and Stack, *The New Haven Laboratory* [1].

neighborhoods and someone choses the Hamden house if it best suits his or her needs. Ultimately, at some price, the house will probably be sold, but not necessarily. It all depends upon what options families have as *they* go about *their* business.

5. Very little happens in the New Haven model simply because time passes. Things happen for the most part only when someone decides to do something.
6. The model appears complicated because so many things are going on. No single piece is particularly complicated, however. In fact, each piece is no more or less complicated, in principle, than the complexity of the decision it is simulating; in practice each piece is considerably less complicated than the actual decision process.

The model, then, is simply all the pieces placed in one arena where they can observe and react to each other. A primary function of the model as a whole is to keep track of what each piece does and to make that knowledge readily available to all the other pieces. Following our example, it remembers that a builder built a house and that a businessman opened a store in northern Hamden, so that when a family looking for a new house "looks" in northern Hamden, it will "see" that these other things have happened and will take them into account.

The Future

Because of our interest in the practical needs of administrators in New Haven, and in order to facilitate comparison of changes in the 1960's with those in the 1970's, we use 1980 as our future date. All of the 1980 predictions contained in this section were obtained by running our model from 1970 (the last "known point") to 1980, making our best guesses about how people are likely to behave during the 1970's. Some of the consequences of our best guesses being wrong will be examined in the next section.

An examination of the 1980 predictions shows a continuation of the relatively larger growth of the suburbs and a decline in the central city's share of virtually everything. The relative decline in the city's share of population and housing units will be far greater, however, than the decline in its share of jobs.

As can be seen in Tables 7-1 and 7-2, the central city population will level off at around 135,000 people.[b] The mix will continue to change, as minorities move in and the native and foreign born population moves out. The percent minority in the central city, which increased from 16 percent to 32 percent between 1960 and 1970, will stand at 48 percent in 1980.

---

[b]We have assumed that the massive demolitions in the central city (7,800 units) of the 1960's will not be repeated in the 1970's.

The influx of minorities will keep up the pressure on the central city housing market, pushing up rents and prices (in real dollars) considerably. Construction of approximately 200 units per year in the outlying tracts will compensate for some of the abandonment in inner-city neighborhoods such as Dixwell and Newhallville.

Underlying the relatively slow growth in total central city employment will be a rather significant shift in its composition. Service and government jobs, which together constituted only 29 percent of the total as recently as 1960, will account for 52 percent by 1980. The central city is turning more and more into a service, office-building complex—a trend that will help it a great deal in its long-term struggle for survival. Were the region's employment base to revert once again to manufacturing, the story could be quite different.

Suburban growth, in contrast, will be supported by a more balanced economy (see Tables 7-1 and 7-3). Manufacturing will hold its own as the bulk of new manufacturing plants locate outside the central city and as old ones relocate there. The population-serving and construction sectors will thrive as well on the general suburban growth.

By 1980, the suburban population, which was roughly equal to the central city population in 1960, will be almost twice as large. The mix of people will stay more or less the same, the only significant change being the increase in minority persons to 6.1 percent of the total (up from 3.8 percent in 1970, representing an absolute increase of 7,400).

The types and cost of housing in which the growing suburban population will live will change significantly. As you might expect, prices will rise. More important, however, is the shift from owned to rental units—mostly apartments. The rising costs of land and labor and construction materials will force builders and planning boards more and more into high-density construction, possibly with a buffer zone of untouched land around it PUD-style[c] to keep the overall densities down. Fully 52 percent of of the units built in the suburbs in the 1970's will be of this variety, up from 43 percent during the 1960's.

Individual towns and neighborhoods will experience quite dramatic shifts. Hamden and Guilford will spurt ahead. The central city neighborhoods of Brookside-Rockview, Whitney, and Fair Haven will witness the kind of minority "take over" that the Hill and Newhallville saw during the 1960's. Suburbs like Branford, Hamden, Guilford, and particularly West Haven will have to learn to live with significant minority concentrations for the first time. Several suburbs will experience substantial expansion of their own, independent employment bases—particularly North Haven and West Haven.

Summarizing, the basic shift toward suburbs that are less and less "sub-urban" shows no signs of letting up. While the central city will continue to

[c]A PUD, or Planned Unit Development, is a form of real estate development in which a relatively large tract of land is planned as a unit, frequently with most of the housing units clustered in a central area surrounded by "natural" woods or fields or lakes.

Table 7-1
Population and Employment by District in 1960, 1970, and 1980[1]

District	*Total Population*			*Percent Minority*			*Total Employment*		
	1960	*1970*	*1980*	*1960*	*1970*	*1980*	*1960*	*1970*	*1980*
Central City									
Brookside-Rockview	9,999	10,293	10,822	17.2	36.5	55.6	6,929	4,646	4,358
Westville	7,573	7,360	7,083	.9	4.0	6.0	154	1,123	1,765
Beaver Hills-Edgewood	15,513	13,240	13,468	5.4	17.3	31.0	3,019	4,138	5,051
Newhallville	9,477	9,122	8,608	43.4	81.9	91.9	810	1,914	2,593
Dixwell	10,230	7,285	6,825	74.1	85.2	93.1	3,902	3,009	2,601
Dwight	6,998	6,594	6,980	22.2	37.0	70.9	2,096	3,757	5,463
Hill	22,726	20,580	20,090	12.0	52.3	72.7	5,275	5,720	6,335
Cent. Bus.	1,292	676	767	8.7	17.3	62.4	23,863	31,705	47,047
Whitney	15,551	14,751	15,372	5.9	15.9	40.3	10,727	9,476	11,727
Wooster Sq.	10,706	4,373	4,414	24.7	37.0	62.1	10,231	6,915	6,368
Fair Haven	19,554	15,793	15,334	5.1	18.5	38.3	8,792	7,393	6,877
Heights	5,672	8,546	13,345	1.0	13.6	29.7	935	2,072	2,805
Fairmont	4,628	5,404	5,125	.6	2.6	2.9	3,830	3,660	3,564
Morris Cove	4,789	6,052	5,592	.0	1.7	2.6	246	721	1,068
Longwharf	1,047	317	294	25.3	4.4	18.3	7,317	6,465	6,918
Central City Total	145,755	130,386	134,118	16.2	31.9	47.7	88,126	92,713	114,539

Suburbs									
Branford	16,609	20,445	25,134	1.0	1.9	4.3	3,582	5,473	6,597
East Haven	21,391	25,162	30,507	.3	.8	2.0	1,588	3,182	4,913
North Haven	15,936	22,151	26,937	1.5	3.1	3.9	9,573	15,464	14,898
Hamden	40,972	48,519	62,703	1.5	4.7	7.3	10,832	15,217	17,630
Woodbridge	5,181	7,739	9,645	1.3	1.9	3.6	399	1,064	2,073
Orange	8,544	13,522	15,789	.3	1.8	1.8	2,513	4,785	5,645
West Haven	42,479	52,239	58,520	2.1	6.2	10.3	8,478	13,371	16,185
Guilford	7,811	12,036	17,483	1.2	3.4	5.7	1,436	2,848	4,738
Suburban Total	158,923	201,813	246,717	1.3	3.8	6.1	38,401	61,404	72,678
Region Total	304,678	332,199	380,835	8.5	14.8	20.7	126,527	154,117	187,217

Source: See Table 4-1.

[1]Totals may not add due to rounding.

Table 7-2
Population, Housing, and Employment for the City in 1960, 1970, and 1980

	1960		*1970*		*1980*	
	Number	*Percent*	*Number*	*Percent*	*Number*	*Percent*
Population						
Age						
0-19	46,422	31.8	42,798	32.8	52,326	39.0
20-39	39,078	26.8	37,168	28.5	36,059	26.9
40-64	42,874	29.4	33,869	26.0	31,321	23.4
65+	17,381	11.9	16,551	12.7	14,412	10.7
Ethnic/Racial						
Native	102,316	70.2	76,343	58.6	63,497	47.3
Foreign	19,798	13.6	12,394	9.5	6,594	4.9
Minority	23,641	16.2	41,649	31.9	64,027	47.7
Education						
< H. S.	105,310	72.3	84,907	65.1	84,030	62.7
= H. S.	23,884	16.4	25,888	19.9	28,873	21.5
> H. S.	16,561	11.4	19,591	15.0	21,215	15.8
Total	145,755	100.0	130,386	100.0	134,118	100.0
Occupied Housing Units[1]						
Tenure						
Own	16,573	33.7	14,816	31.6	14,872	30.6
Rent	32,597	66.3	32,039	68.4	33,738	69.4
Price						
High	7,438	15.1	17,934	38.3	25,671	52.8
Middle	24,317	49.5	17,864	38.1	15,380	31.6
Low	17,416	35.4	11,057	23.6	7,559	15.6
Total	49,171	100.0	46,856	100.0	48,610	100.0
Jobs by Industry						
Non-Durable	14,810	16.8	7,768	8.4	3,781	3.3
Durable	14,349	16.3	8,897	9.6	5,981	5.2
Construct.	4,060	4.6	3,061	3.3	2,892	2.5
Trans.	4,825	5.5	4,504	4.9	3,814	3.3
Comm. and Util.	5,350	6.1	6,737	7.3	8,196	7.2
Wholesale	4,860	5.5	6,014	6.5	6,852	6.0
Retail	10,330	11.7	11,847	12.8	15,612	13.6
F.I.R.E.[2]	5,732	6.5	6,481	7.0	7,486	6.5
Services	16,820	19.1	26,256	28.3	40,865	35.7
Government	6,990	7.9	11,147	12.0	19,060	16.6
Total	88,126	100.0	92,713	100.0	114,539	100.0

Source: See Table 4-1.

[1]The price breakdowns for housing units include both owned and rental units.

[2]Finance, Insurance, and Real Estate.

Table 7-3
Population, Housing, and Employment for the Suburbs in 1960, 1970, and 1980

	1960		*1970*		*1980*	
	Number	*Percent*	*Number*	*Percent*	*Number*	*Percent*
Population						
Age						
0-19	58,203	36.6	72,190	35.8	86,116	34.9
20-39	38,835	24.4	47,817	23.7	61,009	24.7
40-64	47,698	30.0	62,690	31.1	73,548	29.8
65+	14,187	8.9	19,116	9.5	26,044	10.6
Ethnic/Racial						
Native	143,517	90.3	181,022	89.7	220,725	89.5
Foreign	13,262	8.3	13,196	6.5	11,008	4.5
Minority	2,144	1.3	7,595	3.8	14,984	6.1
Education						
< H. S.	102,672	64.6	119,564	59.2	132,717	53.8
= H. S.	32,342	20.4	45,564	22.6	62,731	25.4
> H. S.	23,909	15.0	36,685	18.2	51,269	20.8
Total	158,923	100.0	201,813	100.0	246,717	100.0
Occupied Housing Units[1]						
Tenure						
Own	37,028	79.9	46,054	74.2	55,507	68.0
Rent	9,317	20.1	16,041	25.8	26,105	32.0
Price						
High	8,566	18.5	22,382	36.0	43,967	53.9
Middle	23,169	50.0	26,680	43.0	27,094	33.2
Low	14,610	31.5	13,032	21.0	10,550	12.9
Total	46,345	100.0	62,095	100.0	81,612	100.0
Jobs by Industry						
Non-Durable	4,400	11.5	8,764	14.3	9,690	13.3
Durable	11,551	30.1	16,589	27.0	17,742	24.4
Construct.	2,480	6.5	3,565	5.8	3,463	4.8
Trans.	1,940	5.1	2,551	4.2	3,151	4.3
Comm. and Util.	300	0.8	440	0.7	433	0.6
Wholesale	2,290	6.0	2,919	4.8	3,711	5.1
Retail	6,770	17.6	10,922	17.8	13,100	18.0
F.I.R.E.[2]	790	2.1	1,286	2.1	1,268	1.7
Services	3,300	8.6	6,392	10.4	9,275	12.8
Government	4,580	11.9	7,977	13.0	10,844	14.9
Total	38,401	100.0	61,404	100.0	72,678	100.0

Source: See Table 4-1.

[1]The price breakdowns for housing units include both owned and rental units.

[2]Finance, Insurance, and Real Estate.

specialize in minority people, rental housing and service jobs, the suburbs will get their share of all three and will continue to see expansion in their native populations, in jobs of all kinds, and in some single family home construction.

Testing the Assumptions

Our forecast for 1980 is based on a large number of assumptions about how people will behave. Since, in fact, future behavior is uncertain, and since our understanding of the past and present is less than perfect, it is helpful to the consumer of a model's output to know which assumptions play a key role in the model and how the forecast might be altered if the assumptions prove wrong. Actual users of the model can, of course, check a wide variety of assumptions by sitting at a console and changing them—one at a time or in combination. In this brief section we will only be able to examine a few, and these at a fairly high level of aggregation. We will divide our assumptions and our discussion of them into two parts—assumptions about flows across the region's boundaries and assumptions about phenomena that are largely internal to the region.

Our procedure for testing assumptions will be the same in each case. The model is first run from 1970 to 1980 with our best guess regarding all of the assumptions about how people will behave. One or more changes are then made in the assumptions, and a new run is made from 1970 to 1980. The differences between our best-guess, or "Base Run," and the "experimental" run suggest how sensitive the functioning of the region is to unanticipated changes in behavior. The reader must constantly keep in mind that comparisons are being made between two 1980 predictions, not between 1970 and 1980. Thus a drop in the net in-migration of minorities will lead to a *lower* 1980 estimate of the total minority population, but the figure will still be *higher* than it was in 1970—that is, the minority population will still grow through natural increase and some migration, but at a slower rate.

Flows Across the Boundaries

Particularly troublesome are assumptions about how households and businessmen in other regions will respond to changes in New Haven and about how green their New Haven counterparts will view pastures elsewhere. The reality is that each region is "competing" for jobs and people with each other region. We have as yet no way of simulating the details of that competition and the corresponding migration flows. We must, therefore, estimate what the flows will be, based on past experience, and make some adjustments for known conditions in New Haven. Two questions predominate: (1) will minority households continue to be attracted to New Haven as they have been since World War II, and (2) will the employment base continue to grow as it has during the past twenty years? We have assumed so far that, in both cases, the answer is "yes" and that changes are slow and continuous. We will now examine what is likely to happen if we are wrong.

In Table 7-4 we present the effect on our 1980 predictions of reducing the

Table 7-4
Effect of Reducing New Migration of Minorities to Zero

	Central City in 1980			*Suburbs in 1980*		
	Base Run	*Run With Zero Net Minority Migration*	*% Diff.*	*Base Run*	*Run With Zero Net Minority Migration*	*% Diff.*
Total Population	134,118	132,559	– 1.2%	246,717	247,225	+ .2%
No. Min.	64,027	54,593	–14.7%	14,984	9,911	–33.9%
% Min.	47.7%	41.2%		6.1%	4.0%	
Total Households	48,610	48,423	– .4%	81,612	81,796	+ .2%
Total Occupied Housing Units	48,610	48,423	– .4%	81,612	81,796	+ .2%
% Renter Occ.	69.4%	69.4%		32.0%	31.5%	

net migration of minorities to zero. In the "experimental" run, the decrease in the net flow of minorities is counterbalanced by an increase in the net flow of native and foreign born households, so that the total levels of in- and out-migration remain unchanged. The results are not too surprising—a drop in minority persons of about 15 percent in the central city and 34 percent in the suburbs. The suburban drop is greater in percentage terms as fewer minorities put less pressure on marginal neighborhoods in inner suburban communities. The net effect on the central city is to drop the minority percentage from 48 percent to 41 percent.

This particular experiment shows clearly the strength of natural increase as a cause of growth. By 1970, the New Haven minority population was large enough to sustain an increase in the number of minorities in the region from 49,000 in 1970 to 65,000 in 1980 with no net in-migration.

The effect on the housing stock is negligible, since, in the experiment, the decrease in minorities is compensated by an increase in native and foreign born households to keep the total constant. A close look at the price structure of housing in some communities (not presented in the table) shows a reduced pressure on mid-priced units as the number of middle-class households bailing out of the central city declines. Also, the reduced "turmoil" in the system leads to slightly lower demand for construction and fewer vacant units.

In order to test the sensitivity of our assumption about employment growth, we increased the growth rate of total employment by 25 percent across the board. The results can be seen in Table 7-5. Employment grows in both the city

Table 7-5
Effect of Increasing the Rate of Employment Growth for all Industries by 25%

	Central City in 1980			*Suburbs in 1980*		
	Base Run	*Run With 25% Inc. In Empl. Growth*	*% Diff.*	*Base Run*	*Run With 25% Inc. In Empl. Growth*	*% Diff.*
Total Population	134,118	134,397	+ .2%	246,717	259,696	+5.3%
% Min.	47.7%	47.2%		6.1%	5.6%	
Total Households	48,610	48,937	+ .7%	81,612	85,577	+4.9%
Total Occupied Housing Units	48,610	48,937	+ .7%	81,612	85,577	+4.9%
% Renter Occ.	69.4%	69.7%		32.0%	33.2%	
Total Jobs	114,539	120,378	+5.1%	72,678	76,055	+4.6%
Mfg.	9,762	10,266	+5.2%	27,432	28,758	+4.8%
Serv. & Gov't.	59,925	63,086	+5.3%	20,119	20,898	+3.9%

and the suburbs, the city benefiting from the growth in service and government employment. Most of the increase in population occurs in the suburbs where vacant land for new (increasingly rental) units is available. Not visible in these aggregates is a shift in the mix of households and population caused by the increase in jobs. The opening up of new employment opportunities places a greater emphasis on in-migration as a source of population and household growth, and thereby increases somewhat the proportion of younger households that move into the area. They, in turn, bring their children with them, expanding significantly the number of persons less than 20 years of age. A relatively modest growth in total households, therefore, leads to a somewhat greater growth in total population.

Internal Uncertainties

Though none of the fairly drastic changes in assumptions we have made regarding the flows of minorities and jobs across New Haven's boundaries is very probable, they do highlight the importance of knowing how effectively New Haven will "compete" for jobs and people outside the region. Not to be overlooked, however, are our assumptions about what will happen inside the boundaries. We have conducted a number of experiments that test how sensitive our predictions are to changes in preferences on the part of households and builders and planning boards.

One of the greatest internal uncertainties surrounds the rate at which individuals—particularly young and old ones—will form separate households rather than living with their relatives. In Chapter 4 we indicated that this tendency is increasing over time. The question is: How fast? To give some feeling for the lack of knowledge in this area, in 1972, the Census Bureau[d] forecasted headship rates for the United States to 1980. By 1973 their forecasts for 1980 had already been exceeded in several instances. If the 1970-1973 experience continues, the number of new households formed in the United States during the decade could be 20 million, or almost 50 percent higher than estimates made as recently as 1972.

To see what would happen in New Haven if headship rates increased more rapidly than we anticipate, we doubled the rate of headship increase. The effect, shown in Table 7-6, is nontrivial. The most obvious effect is an increase in construction—mostly in the suburbs. More households need more housing units; in New Haven's already tight housing market that implies building. The increased headship rates, and the corresponding decrease in the number of people living in each unit, leads to a thinning out of the central city population as fewer people occupy the same housing stock. The suburbs gain people as more and more of the new households choose to live outside the city limits—particularly the younger ones. And a larger percentage of the new households prefer, or perhaps can only afford, apartments, increasing the pressure on rental construction.

Table 7-6
Effect of Doubling the Rate of Increase in Headship Rates

	Central City in 1980			*Suburbs in 1980*		
	Base Run	*Run With Headship Increase*	*% Diff.*	*Base Run*	*Run With Headship Increase*	*% Diff.*
Total Population	134,118	121,846	−9.2%	246,717	256,844	+ 4.1%
% Min.	47.7%	48.2%		6.1%	6.4%	
Total Households	48,610	49,453	+1.7%	81,612	90,669	+11.1%
Total Occupied Housing Units	48,610	49,453	+1.7%	81,612	90,669	+11.1%
% Renter Occ.	69.4%	69.7%		32.0%	35.6%	

A number of other "internal" experiments produced quite predictable results, and are not worth describing in detail. A shift in the preference of households for more rental units, for example, led to an increase in the level of apartment construction by about the right amount. A debate is now in process in Guilford regarding the rate at which the town, which is largely undeveloped, is to grow. The debate centers around an ordinance that would increase the minimum acreage for a housing unit from one and one-half to two and one-half acres, effectively halting all but the most expensive construction. We over-simulated

[d]See U.S. Census Bureau [2].

the effect of such an ordinance by halting all construction in Guilford to see what would happen. While the effect on Guilford was dramatic, the effect on the overall development of the region was negligible. Builders looked elsewhere for land, and found it.

In a similar vein, but with very different implications, we did an experiment in the central city to see what would have happened if Mayor Lee and his administration had not initiated the massive renewal effort of the early and mid 1960's. In particular, we ran the model without the demolition of approximately 5,000 units and construction of approximately 4,000 units in their place during the 1960 to 1967 period. An understanding of the results of this experiment does require some detailed comparisons, presented in Table 7-7. Relative to what

Table 7-7
Effect of No Demolitions on the Evolution of New Haven from 1960 to 1967

	Central City in 1967			*Suburbs in 1967*		
	1967 Base Run	*1967 Run w. No. Demo.*	*% Diff.*	*1967 Base Run*	*1967 Run w. No. Demo.*	*% Diff.*
Total Population	132,660	140,949	+6.2%	190,705	182,050	−4.5%
% Min.	26.6%	25.9%		2.0%	1.4%	
Total Households	46,451	48,923	+5.3%	58,814	56,393	−4.1%
Total Occupied Housing Units	46,451	48,923	+5.3%	58,814	56,393	−4.1%
% Renter Occ.	66.1%	65.6%		22.6%	22.5%	
Vacant Units	1,293	1,415	+9.4%	1,507	1,451	−3.7%

actually happened, under the no-renewal policy the city would have gained housing units and households and people as more units were left on the market. The number of vacant units would have gone up as well. Mayor Lee also stimulated a significant amount of construction in the suburbs.

In another round of experiments we explored our assumptions about the tendency of manufacturing establishments to locate near their work force. The results are all quite regular and predictable. As the necessity to be near the geographical center of the labor market decreases, the propensity of manufacturers to locate in the suburbs increases, all other things being equal. Dropping the need for proximity to the labor force to zero increases manufacturing employment in the suburbs by approximately 10 percent over the Base Run during the ten year period from 1970 to 1980.

Conclusions

Now the true behavioral nature of our model is seen. The total model is simply a meeting ground for different kinds of people engaged in a variety of activities. It permits each person to "observe" the behavior of the others and respond accordingly. It is the set of responses that cause change; very few changes take place simply because time passes.

A run to 1980 based on our best guess about how each type of person will behave in the 1970's reveals a continuation of the pattern that began around 1960. The suburbs will grow at a relatively rapid pace on all fronts and will become increasingly less dependent upon the central city as a place of employment, for all the reasons given in Chapters 4 through 6. The population of the central city, in contrast, will stabilize around 135,000 people,[e] 48 percent of whom will be minorities. Total central city employment will grow slowly, but the mix will change quite a bit, shifting out of manufacturing and into the service and government sectors.

Perhaps the most striking thing that emerges from observing the effects of significant changes in our assumptions is that not one of the changes alters substantially the basic shift toward a cluster of increasingly independent, suburban communities. The rates and magnitudes and exact locations at which this shift will take place are affected, to be sure, by changes in the rate of employment growth and changes in preference of different groups for different life styles. But the basic trend persists. Its implications may be profound for policy-makers at all levels, and for the administrators in New Haven whose needs we are trying to satisfy. That is the subject of the next chapter.

---

[e]The reader should keep in mind that the population figures in our work do not include people living in group quarters. People living in group quarters numbered about 9,000 in 1970.

References

1. Birch, Atkinson, Sandström, and Stack. *The New Haven Laboratory.* Lexington, Mass.: Lexington Books, D.C. Heath & Co., 1974.

2. U.S. Bureau of the Census. "Demographic Projections of the United States," *Current Population Reports,* Series P-25, No. 476, p. 9. Washington, D.C.: Government Printing Office, February 1972.

8 Conclusion

Emerging from the behavior of households and builders and bankers and planners and people generally is a more general theme—the gradual re-emergence of the communities surrounding the central core as independent entities with social and economic lives of their own. People are choosing to live in neighborhoods more because of the neighborhoods' physical and social properties and less because of their accessibility to place of work—the main determinant of location between 1800 and 1950. With the advent of the interstate highway system and easy access to air freight terminals, businessmen are doing the same thing with their plants and stores and offices. The central city is no longer the predominant spawning ground for new businesses; they are springing up everywhere.

The central city is changing in the process. It is holding its own in terms of jobs by specializing in the kind of services that require a central location. It is losing population and changing its mix of population dramatically, the influx of minority persons being a principal cause. As did other ethnic/racial groups before them, the minority population is beginning to move into the inner suburban neighborhoods at an increasing rate, bringing the problems of race and poverty to towns that have not experienced them in the recent past. The out-movement of minorities is being felt far more in some communities, such as West Haven and Hamden, than in others such as Orange and Woodbridge, which have managed to maintain the image that most people conjure up when they think of suburbia. It is an increasingly archaic image for suburbs in general.

We have made these observations for New Haven. There are several indications that the same observations could be made elsewhere as well. The analysis of 120 SMSA's presented in Chapter 2 suggests that regions of all sizes are undergoing much the same kinds of transitions, the larger ones being farther along than the smaller ones. The figures on locations of employment and commuting patterns for New Haven are not significantly different from the figures for all SMSA's of comparable size, and the direction of the trends is certainly the same.

As another partial check on the generality of our New Haven findings, the entire New Haven structure is being applied in the Houston/Galveston region in Texas—a young and rapidly growing metropolitan area. The work in Houston is far from complete, but it is already clear that the fundamental urban phenomena in Houston are the same as in New Haven and that the basic outward expansion of economic activity and population is taking place rapidly. One of the problems in observing this trend in Houston is the tendency of the city to annex any adjacent territory that shows signs of life—a privilege granted by state law. If the 1940 central city boundary could be superimposed on present-day Houston, however, many of the statements made about New Haven would be equally true—the influx of minorities, the specialization of the core in service and office jobs, the rapid expansion of jobs and population outside the core, and the increasing tendency for most people to live and work without reference to "downtown."

At a slightly higher level of aggregation, the counties surrounding Houston offer a direct parallel to the suburbs of New Haven. One after another, Montgomery, Brazoria, Chambers and Fort Bend Counties are announcing the development of complete new towns in the 50,000 to 100,000 population range, and jobs to go with them.

Turning in still another direction, the 900 interviews conducted by Coleman and Rainwater[a] in Boston and Kansas City indicate, time and again, the frustration with congested urban life and the strong desire to move away from it and into the suburbs at the first opportunity. As they put it:

> If our findings from Boston and Kansas City are typical for the nation's metropolitan areas, then a very large percentage of middle-income families who still live in older central-city areas, or in industrial satellite neighborhoods, are dissatisfied with their housing and especially its setting. They are extremely eager to move to greener, more suburban areas. They feel "behind the times" in their housing and want to catch up. This thrust toward housing change could not have been revealed by the 1970 Census data. Projections of housing needs through to 1980 which do not take into account these attitudes toward present housing and a desire for a change have missed a major ingredient in the picture of demand and need.

These bits and pieces of evidence scarcely prove that the experience in New Haven is typical, but that experience at least does not seem to contradict what others are beginning to observe in metropolitan areas across the country. If it were a general pattern for even, say, the older, larger urban areas, its significance could be very profound indeed, for the forces lying behind the shift toward more independent, outlying communities are very strong. Referring back to Chapter 1, collectively these forces are like a large pendulum that will be difficult to deflect, much less arrest. Not even significant changes in basic assumptions have much effect. Certainly there are no federal or state programs on the horizon that are of the magnitude required to alter the pattern.

The implications of a new kind of growth are wide ranging. The present census definition of a metropolitan area makes no sense, for example. The Census Bureau now defines a metropolitan area as a core city and that collection of communities that, among other things, send 15 percent or more of their

---

[a]See Birch et al. [1].

residents into the central city each day to work. Increasingly, out-lying communities will develop into urban-looking areas. They will, however, be employing their residents directly or sending them to other nearby communities–not to the central city–for work. As a result, these outlying communities will not be included within the boundaries of metropolitan areas, and will not be called "urban." The present definition of a metropolitan area will thus bear little relationship to the true phenomenon of metropolitan growth and will substantially understate its magnitude.

As communities become more self-sufficient over a wider geographical area, the concept of mass transit–at least as traditionally conceived in terms of radial spokes leading to a central core on grade-separated rights-of-way–will make little sense. People will wish to travel increasingly shorter distances from many points in an urban area to many other points. A resident of North Haven, for example, might work in Hamden or North Haven or Branford and will be less and less likely to work in New Haven City. The high-density corridors, upon which most rapid rail transit systems depend for break even volume, will simply not exist. The automobile has been the predominant solution to providing transportation in a multi-point grid system–a fact to which residents of Los Angeles and Pheonix and Houston can readily testify. It is an increasingly unattractive solution, however, and other solutions may be necessary. Whatever they are, to be realistic, they will have to look like and act like an automobile on a road network.

The movement of the poor and the minorities out of the more depressed central city neighborhoods and into surrounding communities has, in general, not been compensated by a corresponding influx. The inevitable consequence of this movement is the abandonment of central city housing units in poorer neighborhoods. For some time, this abandonment has been viewed as a "problem."

Indeed, if one takes the position of a central city mayor or a resident in one of the neighborhoods experiencing the phenomenon, abandonment does cause problems. This is the viewpoint historically taken by urban analysts and politicians and has led to such programs as Model Cities.

Ignoring geography for a minute, and looking instead at people–poor people in particular–the very process that causes abandonment is the same one whereby poor households move into newer neighborhoods near better schools and better jobs. Looked at from the perspective of poor persons as a group, the more abandonment that is observed in a city, the more likely it is that poor people are able to find and enjoy better opportunities. In short, abandonment is a healthy sign.

The middle ground between these two positions, of course, is that neighborhoods experiencing abandonment should be helped in whatever way possible to ease the burden of transition. Such a set of activities should not be confused, however, with the notion of rebuilding or maintaining these neighborhoods as they once were. All of the evidence from New Haven suggests that this is easily the equivalent of standing on the shore and telling the tide not to come in. To hold forth the hope of restoration and economic prosperity to the residents of a presently deteriorating central city neighborhood–in the interest of encouraging them to stay there–is a malicious policy indeed. Far more useful would be an approach that treated poor people as people, not as occupiers of dwelling units, and that assisted them in any way possible to search for and capitalize upon opportunities wherever they can be found–to move with the tide, in effect, rather than against it.

Thus far we have been addressing ourselves primarily to a broad range of issues that concern the designers of urban programs at the local, state, and federal levels of government. These are the "clients" to whom most studiers of urban areas have addressed themselves, implicitly or otherwise. Yet it is clear to us from our observations in previous chapters that most of the changes taking place in the region are the result of the actions of many individuals–acting privately and more particularly in their roles as administrators of land development firms, banks, welfare agencies, manufacturing plants, schools, and so forth. Though none of the activities of an individual administrator, taken by itself, appears as important as the programs of the planner in explaining urban change, collectively these activities are of a much larger magnitude, and dominate the urban change process.

The question arises: Should not the urban analyst be equally, if not more, interested in working with individual administrators in a region, assisting them in making changes within their own organizations that will keep those organizations healthy? Is not the health of the region strongly dependent, after all, on the health of its parts? We have decided that, in fact, it is, and have chosen to devote a substantial portion of our energies to working with administrators in New Haven to develop methods for assessing the implications of the changes that seem to be taking place.

Our work with organizations has just begun, and it is too early to report any specific results or implications. That is the purpose of a subsequent publication, as indicated in the Preface. Enough has been done, however, to suggest the flavor of things to come.

Many administrators, for example, set up their organizations in the past to capitalize upon the centrality and significance of the core city. Retailers located major stores there. Banks established their main offices there, and only recently began reaching into the outlying territory with branches. Utilities located their main facilities there. Government agencies located their offices and public-access facilities (such as welfare offices and health clinics) there. Museums and symphony orchestras built their main buildings there.

What is happening in each case, of course, is that the central location no longer has the value it did as recently as 15 years ago. This has put a great deal of pressure on administrators of all kinds to reestablish the balance within their own organizations to reflect the balance in the world around them. Stores must move to suburban shopping centers. Banks must significantly increase the commercial lending authority of their branch managers and add branches as fast as possible before new territory is occupied by others. Utilities must find ways to increase, at considerable expense, the networks of mains and wires and pumping stations through which they deliver their products. Welfare officials can no longer assume that all potential clients are within walking distance of one or two central offices; the poor are everywhere now. Directors of museums and orchestras hear increasing complaints about hub caps being stolen and patrons being robbed in parking lots and wonder how to offset the gradual attrition in attendance and financial support.

All the while, administrators in the outlying communities are experiencing the opposite side of the coin. Quiet communities whose populations have remained relatively stable since the agricultural decline of the 19th century are suddenly experiencing sharp increases in requests for building permits and are doubling in population every five or ten years. Town officials become perplexed by rising tax rates in the face of apparent prosperity—the economics of community growth are not as favorable as many had expected, if they had thought about it at all. Small store owners are eclipsed overnight by large shopping centers and big discount houses. Car dealers and suppliers of building materials must scramble to keep up. School superintendents must grapple with the tradeoff between a rising population and a declining birth rate and family size, and decide how many new classrooms to ask the voters to finance over the next ten years.

In several instances, we have started working closely with individual organizations, translating our findings about the region into the practical language of branches and pumping stations and classrooms. It is a complicated task, requiring a detailed understanding of the process by which each organization interacts with its customers and its suppliers and its labor force. It is nevertheless the kind of task that each organization must undertake if the region is to pass through the transition period efficiently.

We have only observed a single city in depth thus far. While there are indications that phenomena similar to those found in New Haven can be found elsewhere as well, nothing approaching a general theory exists yet. Each area still contains its own mysteries that must be understood before actions can be taken on its behalf.

A striking thing about New Haven, however, is the strength and energy of the underlying dynamics relative to the size of the programs under the control of those whose job it is to govern and administer. New Haven is going to do pretty much what it wants to do, regardless of who is in the White House or the State House or the Mayor's Office. Even in his "massive" renewal efforts of the 1950's and 1960's, Richard Lee was demolishing many housing units that our simulation suggests would have been abandoned anyway. Even he was not substantially altering the movement of the tides. In fact, it could be claimed that his greatest skill as a politician was sensing that movement accurately and joining forces with it. Many others have not learned the lesson as well as he.

If we are to invest our financial and social capital well over the next several years—and the sums will be large—we must have a better understanding of what is causing change. We desperately need the general theory, or understanding, for which our analysis of New Haven can only serve as a single observation. The time has arrived, in short, when we can no longer afford not to start counting teeth. We must do so quickly if we are to create and preserve a decent urban environment in which to live.

References

1. Birch, Atkinson, Clay, Coleman, Frieden, Friedlander, Rainwater, and Teplitz. *Toward Housing Goals for the United States: Concepts, Methods, and Measures.* MIT-Harvard Joint Center for Urban Studies, 1973.

Appendixes

Appendix A
1960 Census Tracts in Districts[a] and Towns of the New Haven SMSA

District	*1960 Census Tract(s)*
1. Brookside-Rockview	12, 13
2. Westville	10, 11
3. Beaver Hills-Edgwood	14, 9, 8
4. Newhallville	15
5. Dixwell	16
6. Dwight	7
7. Hill	3, 4, 5, 6
8. Central Business District	1
9. Whitney	17, 18, 19, 20
10. Wooster Sq.	21, 22
11. Fair Haven	23, 24, 25
12. Heights	26
13. Fairmont	27
14. Morris Cove	28
15. Long Wharf	2
16. Branford	29, 30, 31, 32
17. East Haven	33, 34, 35, 36
18. North Haven	37, 38, 39
19. Hamden	40, 41, 42, 43, 44, 45, 46, 47, 48
20. Woodbridge	49
21. Orange	50
22. West Haven[b]	51, 52, 54, 55, 56, 57, 58, 59, 60, 61
23. Guilford	62

[a]The "District" level of aggregation within the central city has been defined as aggregations of census tracts that correspond roughly to the outlying towns, thus rounding out a set of geographical units intermediate between the whole region and the individual census tract.

[b]Tract 53 is a hospital, and has been omitted from our analysis.

Appendix B
The New Haven Model

In the body of this book we have deliberately treated the New Haven model as though it were a black box, cradled in and operated upon by a series of laboratory instruments. Now we will probe inside the box somewhat and mention a few things about the instruments.

The process of evolution of the model has also been a process of increasing complexity, as one might expect. We developed a modular structure to deal with that complexity. As in the laboratory, no single module is that complex; it is their combination into an operating structure that gives the appearance of complexity. Our goal in this overview is to describe the structure and how it operates.

The first thing to understand about the New Haven Model is that it is not based on any particular algorithm or formal structure such as linear programming or dynamic programming. Rather, it is a series of routines, each of which observes the state of the region at the instant it is called upon, and, using parameters at its disposal, decides to do something. The process might be diagrammed as in Figure B-1. In the Common Base are stored all the values of the variables that describe the state of the region—numbers of households, people, jobs, houses, acres of land, and so forth by type and by census tract. Once each year, each routine updates the common base from its perspective. The user, through the use of switches, can control the parameters.

Each of the substantive routines simulates the behavior of a specific group of people—households, builders, businessmen, zoning boards, movers, migrants, college graduates, mothers, and so forth. Each set of actors in each census tract looks at the world (the Common Base), decides what he or she will do this year, and does it. For example, a builder on the west side of town might look at the rate at which the area has been growing, the vacancy rates by type of unit, the availability and cost of land in each neighborhood, and the existing zoning and decide how many foundations to lay this year and what to build on them. The result of his actions is recorded in the Common Base as an increase in the number of available units of the type he built, in the neighborhood(s) he built them in, lagged by the number of years he took to complete the project if it was a big one. This process, across all actors, generates a fair amount of detail and some routines are needed to do "accounting." They keep track of which people are living in which households, which households are living in which housing units, how much land is being used up by builders, and so forth.

The model is thus, with some obvious limitations, literally a simulation of the behavior of the actors in the region. The two obvious exceptions are: (1) each actor makes decisions only once a year, rather than every day or every hour, and (2) the actors decide sequentially rather than simultaneously within any year.

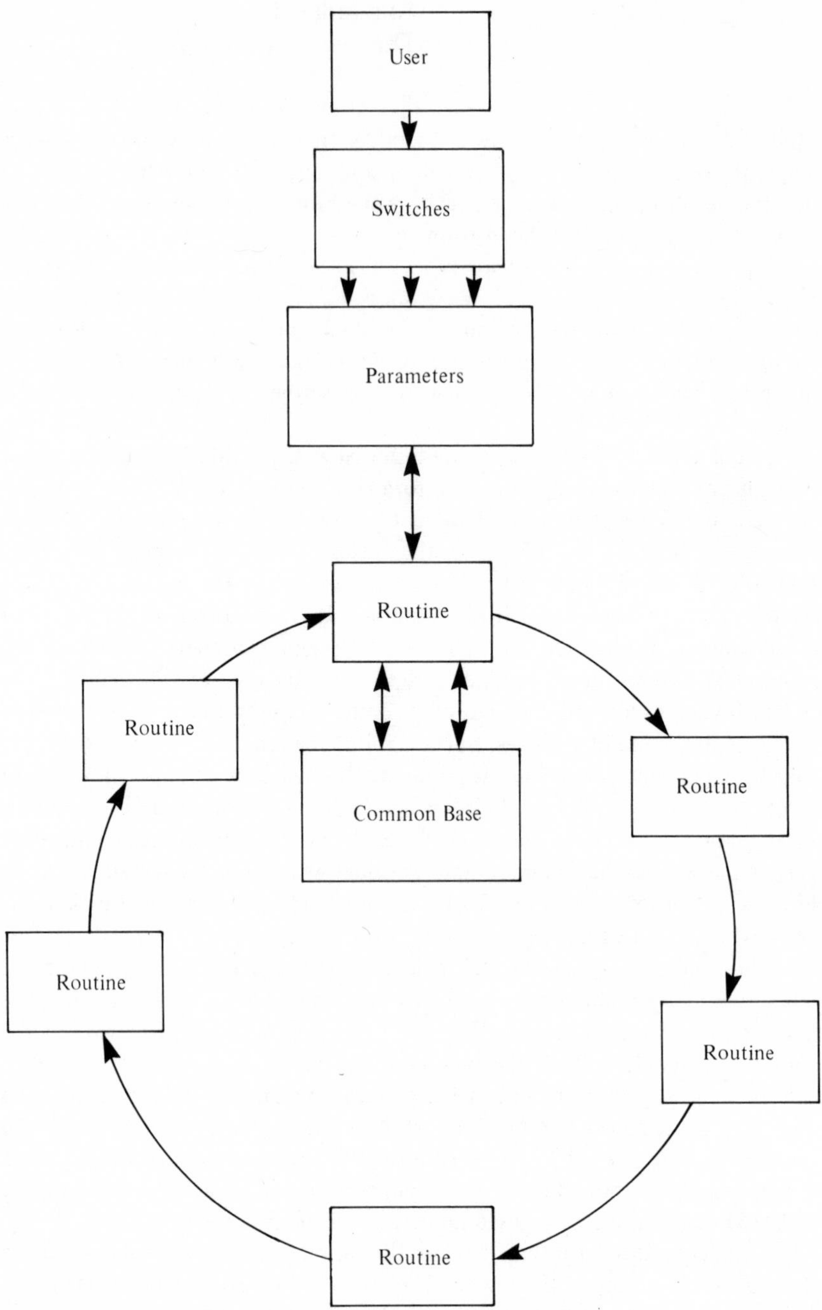

Figure B-1 Abstract Diagram of New Haven Model

Given the lags in the real system, we do not feel that these are serious problems in most cases.

A forecast produced by the model is thus not a direct extrapolation of objects themselves, but is the net result of all the decisions made by all the individuals and all the groups in the social system over time. Very little happens in the New Haven Model simply because time passes. Things happen only when someone decides to do something. For this reason, we call it a *behavioral* model as distinct from a *statistical* model that extrapolates numbers of people and housing units and jobs over time.

There is, in principle, no limit to the number of routines that can be put in the annual loop, nor to the nature of the operations that any individual routine can perform, so long as it does not disturb the structure of the Common Base during a run. Between runs, the Common Base and/or the file of parameters are, also, in principle, infinitely changeable.

Each routine is capable of affecting each other routine through its effect on the Common Base. For example, when a builder builds a speculative, single-family unit, his action is recorded, and movers looking for new houses of that type will take the new house into account when they move. Similarly, when a plant lays off several thousand employees, as happened in the late 1960's in New Haven, people in the same occupational categories as those of the workers laid off will find it harder to find jobs and are more likely to become unemployed. That, in turn, will affect the likelihood that they will migrate elsewhere and that others like themselves will migrate into New Haven. These are the "feedback loops" mentioned so often in the literature on dynamic modeling. The New Haven Model contains virtually an unlimited number of them, although few are direct. Most occur through changes in the Common Base.

Common Base

As indicated above, the Common Base contains all the variables the model keeps track of over time. The most important ones are defined in Table B-1. These variables are stored for each census tract (or district) and/or the region as a whole. The output of the model is simply the Common Base at the point in time when the user chooses to stop the simulation. Not all of the Common Base is stored for display for efficiency reasons, but it could be.

Parameters

The creator of each routine specifies the number and values of the parameters he wishes to use in his routine. These parameters are packed into the model's main data file prior to running it, and are available upon request. They can be altered

Table B-1
Important Variables in the Common Base

Variable	*Description*
NH	Number of households, by type of household by type of housing unit by tract.
POP	Number of people, by type by tract
N	Number of households, by type by tract.
RJ	Number of jobs, by type by district.
REST	Number of manufacturing establishments, by type and district.
STOC	Number of housing units, by tenure and price by tract.
TOCC	Number of occupied housing units, by tenure and price by tract.
VAC	Number of vacancies, by type by tract.
CON	Annual construction, by type of unit by tract.
DEADNH	Number of households dissolved (primarily through death) per year, by type of household head by type of housing unit by tract.
NEWHH	Number of new households per year created by natural increase, by type by tract.
IMIG	Number of households in-migrating per year, by type by tract of arrival.
OMIG	Number of households out-migrating per year, by type by tract of departure.
ARRIVERS	Number of local movers arriving in each tract, by type of household.
LEAVERS	Number of local movers leaving each tract, by type of household.
EXCESS	Excess demand for housing units per year, by type of household by type of unit for each tract.
UNEMUS	U.S. unemployment rate.
UNEMME	Metropolitan unemployment rate.
RAINTE	Interest rate on Mortgages.
USJ	Jobs by type in the U.S.
UNEMO	Unemployment rate by occupation for the region.
UNEMI	Unemployment rate by industry for the region.
UNEMP	Unemployment rate by type of person for the region.
HCH	Change in number of households, by type in each tract, from the previous year.
LAND	Acres of land, by use by tract.
MAXDEN	The maximum density at which builders are permitted (through zoning) to build in each tract for a particular year.
DSTNCE	Average access time from any district to any other district in the region.

at the beginning of the run and, in some cases, during execution, by the user through switches.

Routines

A list and brief description of the basic routines in the model is presented in Table B-2. While each of the routines interacts with all the others through the Common Base, it is useful to diagram some of the major flows between particular common arrays and particular routines. This is done in Figure B-2. The routines are in boxes; the arrays in circles. As can be seen, the flows back and forth between routines are substantial, even at this rather high level of aggregation.

Supporting Models

The iterative nature of our approach puts a high premium on being able to run the model over and over again—literally hundreds of times a week if necessary. For many purposes, the whole model is not needed, and a smaller version will suffice—reducing the running time and cost. Reduction in size can be achieved in two ways: (1) reducing the number of geographic areas, and (2) reducing the number of routines.

On the geographic side we have developed two supporting models: the SMSA Model and the 7-TRACT Model. The SMSA Model simulates all the changes that take place at the regional level—migration, job growth, housing construction, and so forth—ignoring the intraregional location of these phenomena. The 7-TRACT Model is a complete replica of the full model with the exception that it contains only seven census tracts, reducing the size considerably. The SMSA Model is used to calibrate regional totals. The 7-TRACT Model is used to work out the detailed logical flows between the routines. Either model can be run independently. Each has its own data base and its own display systems.

Frequently it is desirable to be able to isolate a single routine or group of routines to see how it (or they) are performing. This can be done either by bypassing the other routines or by creating dummy routines that interpolate between known data points, thus approximating the real world. A good example of this type of package is MOVE. The MOVE package is similar to the main model up through the MOVER routine. It then bypasses CLEAR and HOUSE and relies upon an interpolative BUILDER to keep the balance within the housing stock correct. It thereby simulates the intraregional migration without imposing any housing constraints. In a similar fashion, JOBMAC and JOBMIC can be run independently. In each case, the size and running time of the reduced package are considerably smaller than those for the full model, permitting much more flexible and frequent access.

Table B-2
Major Routines in the New Haven Model

Name	*Function(s)*
EXEC	Reads in the initial conditions and parameters, sets up the timing sequence, calls the major functional routines, and handles some of the interactive communication with the user regarding whether or not to run again, and if so, under what circumstances.
SWITCH	Interrogates the user to determine which, if any, conditions or parameters should be changed for the up-coming run. This can be done in a bulk-input mode for the expert or in a very chatty dialogue for the inexperienced user.
VITAL	Computes the basic shifts that take place within the population as a result of births, deaths, marriage, aging, and assimilation from one ethnic and/or educational group into another.
JOBEXEC	JOBEXEC is an executive routine all its own that parcels out the task of computing the shifts in employment that take place within the region.
JOBMAC	A crude macro model of the U.S. economy that estimates value added and employment, by sector, as well as inflation, interest rate, and unemployment.
JOBREG	Estimates changes in employment in the New Haven region as a whole. It also simulates the regional labor market and determines unemployment rates by occupation, industry, and type of person.
JOBMIC	Determines the location of jobs within the SMSA for each of 10 industries. Treats nondurable and durable manufacturing on an establishment basis, keeping track of births, deaths, movement, expansion and contraction for each of three employment sizes. Eight nonmanufacturing industries are dealt with on a job basis.
MIG	Computes the migration into and out of the region by type of household. Determines the first residential choice of each in-migrant and ascertains the tract from which each out-migrant left.
MAP	Maps back and forth between households and persons, keeping the two consistent and up-to-date.
MOVER	Determines: (1) the odds that each family of each type in each tract will in fact move during the present year, and (2) the most probable tract in which each family will locate, assuming, for the minute, that there are vacancies of the proper sort to move into.
CLEAR	CLEAR examines the residential preferences of all movers, in-migrants, and new households by type of household, type of housing unit desired, and location, and "decides" given the vacancies available, who will get to move into which tract.
HOUSE	HOUSE simulates the details of the housing market within each tract. It conducts the negotiations between renters and landlords, and ultimately decides who gets to live in exactly what kind of housing unit. In the process, it raises rents and prices when demand is excessive and lowers them when demand falls off. Automatic adjustments are made for inflation.

Name	*Function(s)*
BUILDER	BUILDER performs the functions of the building industry. It looks at the unsatisfied demand by tract and type of housing (calculated in CLEAR), the shifts in employment and population, and the level of vacancies, and decides how many housing units of which type to construct in each tract.
ALLMAT	Computes the housing preferences of households searching for new housing.
EARTH	Updates the land use as new construction takes place or as land is taken deliberately from one category and put in another. Also simulates the shifts in zoning ordinances by neighborhood.
PRINT	The bulk of the output from the model is written automatically onto a storage device in the computer for more leisurely examination after the run is completed. The user has the option, however, of obtaining several summary reports directly on the console. PRINT produces these reports.

Operation

All models in the package operate in the same way. All are interactive–the user communicates with the model before, during, and after execution. At the beginning, the user has the option of setting four sets of switches–called DS, OS, IS, and INTERVENTION–that enable him to alter data, output, internal logic, and external events that cannot be predicted within the logical structure of the model.

There is one DS switch for each of the 6,000 parameters. Each parameter switch has a number and can be changed to any desired value at the beginning of a run.

The OS switches are used primarily for debugging[a] purposes. They permit the user to display virtually any of the internal workings of the model during execution. There are 100 OS switches. The IS switches control the internal logic of the model. With proper settings, the user can vary the number of simulated years, can bypass certain routines, can operate the full model as though it were an SMSA model to check regional totals, and so forth. There are 50 IS switches.

The INTERVENTION switches are actually part of a separate routine that permits the user to intervene in the areas of demolition, public housing, and jobs. No model that we know of is rich enough to explain all aspects of urban change. If the unexplainable is left mixed in with the phenomena being explained, at best a fuzzy set of relationships is obtained. We prefer, instead, to acknowledge explicitly that which we cannot explain well, and devote the logic to those aspects of the region that we feel we understand. The INTERVENTION

[a]"Debugging" is a term that has grown out of the computer programming field. It refers to the process by which the programmer isolates and removes logical "bugs" in his code.

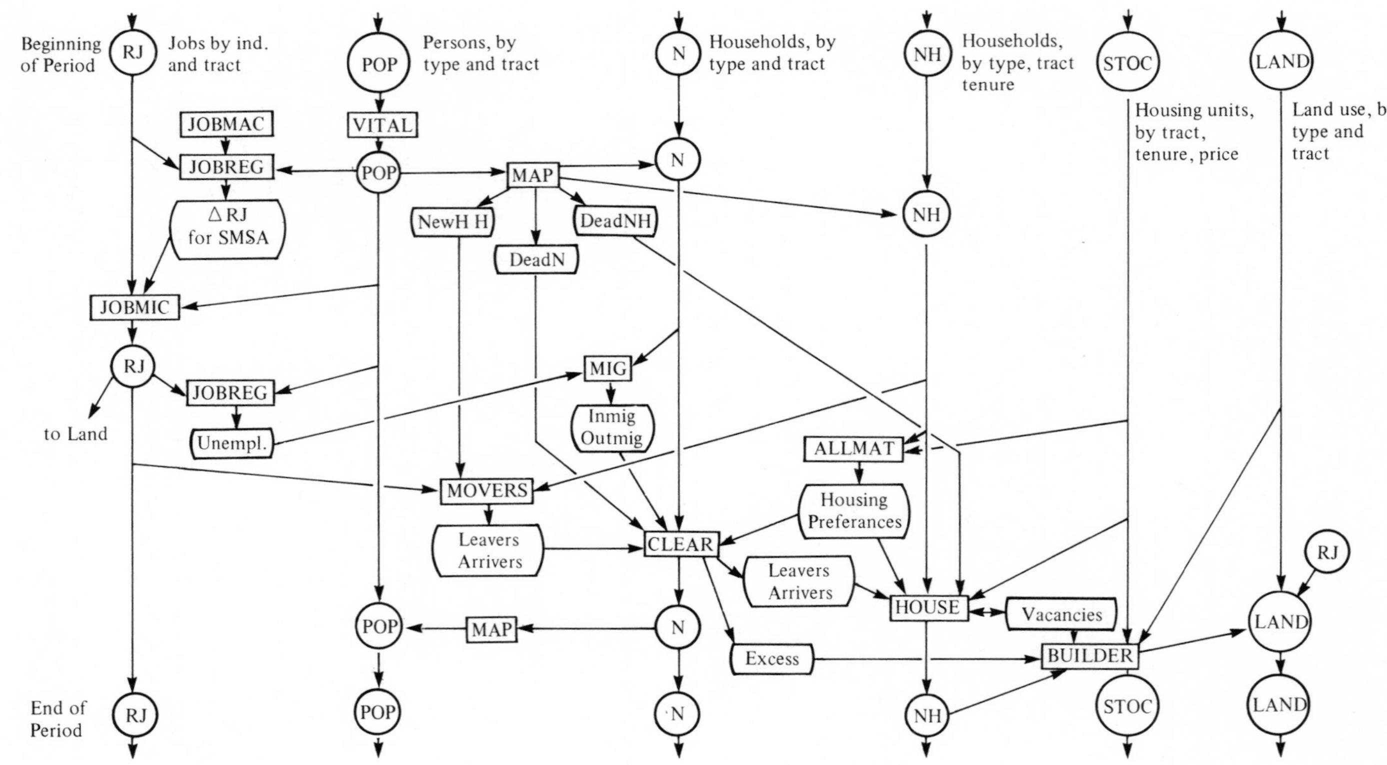

Figure B-2 Major Flows in the New Haven Model

routine performs this function when running over past history by inserting known, unmodeled events. It also permits the user to intervene in future years as a means of testing public policies in the fields of housing and economic development.

Debugging a model as complex as the New Haven Model is no small task. Each routine must be functioning correctly for the other routines to work well. The initial data must be correct and consistent. Furthermore, consistency must be maintained during execution. In our experience, it is virtually impossible to locate a mistake by observing the final result. Too many things could have caused most errors.

One approach to dealing with this complexity is the use of output switches, described above. Frequently, though, it is not clear at the beginning which switch should be turned on. As a further aid to debugging, therefore, we have devised an elaborate system of internal consistency checks within the model itself. Fully 25 percent of the computer code is devoted to these checks. When a test fails, the computation is interrupted, and a message is printed on the user's console indicating the location, nature, and magnitude of the failure. The user then has the option of continuing or terminating, based on his interpretation of the message.

When the model has reached the desired termination year, and passed all its tests, selected portions of the Common Base are dumped into permanent storage, and the laboratory instruments described above take over to dissect the results.

To give the reader a feeling for what an actual run looks like, a sample run (with a number of errors deliberately left in) is included as Figure B-3. Characters typed by the user are underlined.[b]

Instruments

As indicated in Chapter 3, the New Haven Model, and its family of supporting models, constitute a relatively small part of the laboratory in which they were grown. A detailed description of the instruments in that laboratory is provided in *The New Haven Laboratory*.[c] We will attempt in this appendix only to indicate some of the functions that these instruments perform, grouping them under the headings of data reduction, pattern recognition, and verification.

---

[b]For those with an interest in such matters, the present version of the New Haven Model runs on a DEC PDP10-70, consuming about 75,000 words of memory. It averages about one and one-half minutes per simulated year. At off-shift rates, this amounts to about $1.50 for a ten-year simulation.

[c]Birch, Atkinson, Sandström, and Stack, *The New Haven Laboratory*, Lexington, Mass.: Lexington Books, D.C. Heath & Co., 1974.

RUN MODEL

```
CHANGE IS ? YES

HOW MANY ? 1

SWITCH NO. ? 38                          (Incorporates Demolitions)

IS 38 NOW  0  NEW VALUE? 1

MISTAKES ? NO

CHANGE OS ? YES

HOW MANY ? 4

SWITCH NO. ? 21                          (Prints year and "clock" time)

OS 21 NOW  0  NEW VALUE? 1

SWITCH NO. ? 22                          (Prints annual summary)

OS 22 NOW  0  NEW VALUE? 1

SWITCH NO. ? 81                          (Stores job details on disk)

OS 81 NOW  0  NEW VALUE? 1

SWITCH NO. ? 82                          (Stores job details on disk)

OS 82 NOW  0  NEW VALUE? 1

MISTAKES ? NO

CHANGE DS ? NO


DO YOU WANT TO INTERVENE? NO

YEAR = 1961 01:15 32.3
YEAR = 1961
T.POP =  308182.
T.HH =    96991.
T.JOBS =  130687.
UNEMPL. RATE =      0.048

YEAR = 1962 01:18 25.5
YEAR = 1962
T.POP =  309814.
T.HH =    97963.
T.JOBS =  133287.
UNEMPL. RATE =      0.053
```

```
YEAR = 1963 01:20 25.9
YEAR = 1963
T.POP =  312628.
T.HH =   99363.
T.JOBS =  137064.
UNEMPL.  RATE =     0.048

YEAR = 1964 01:22 15.3
YEAR = 1964
T.POP =  317389.
T.HH =  101240.
T.JOBS =  141041.
UNEMPL.  RATE =     0.045

YEAR = 1965 01:24 03.3
YEAR = 1965
T.POP =  318775.
T.HH =  102163.
T.JOBS =  145210.
UNEMPL.  RATE =     0.046

YEAR = 1966 01:25 54.8
MOVERS: DEMO LARGER THAN STOC FOR JH=  1 JP=  1 I=  2
  OK TO GO ON, FIX UP DONE AUTOMATICALLY
MOVERS: DEMO LARGER THAN STOC FOR JH=  1 JP=  2 I=  2
  OK TO GO ON, FIX UP DONE AUTOMATICALLY
MOVERS: DEMO LARGER THAN STOC FOR JH=  1 JP=  3 I=  2
  OK TO GO ON, FIX UP DONE AUTOMATICALLY
YEAR = 1966
T.POP =  322755.
T.HH =  103865.
T.JOBS =  149567.
UNEMPL.  RATE =     0.040

YEAR = 1967 01:27 58.9
MAP: SUM OF NH OVER JH,JP AND N DIFF.     5.232    0.097   23   40
MOVERS: DEMO LARGER THAN STOC FOR JH=  1 JP=   1 I=  2
  OK TO GO ON, FIX UP DONE AUTOMATICALLY
MOVERS: DEMO LARGER THAN STOC FOR JH=  1 JP=   2 I=  2
  OK TO GO ON, FIX UP DONE AUTOMATICALLY
MOVERS: DEMO LARGER THAN STOC FOR JH=  1 JP=   3 I=  2
  OK TO GO ON, FIX UP DONE AUTOMATICALLY
HOUSE SUM OF NH  IS      5.242  N IS      0.107   40   23
TRICK:NH/OLDN     5.242   0.107   40   23       1   4
TRICK:NH/N        5.242   0.107   40   23       1   4
YEAR = 1967
T.POP =  326756.
T.HH =  105663.
T.JOBS =  154106.
UNEMPL.  RATE =     0.039

EXIT
```

Figure B-3 Sample Run of Full Model

Reducing Data

The gathering and reduction of data is extremely tedious and time consuming in practice, but simple in concept. Much of the gathering has nothing to do with computers and involves meeting with potential data providers, digging out old tables, interviewing builders, reviewing past surveys, conducting surveys, and so forth.

As this so-called "raw data" begins to accumulate, a number of things become clear. First, only a small portion of it is directly useful, and that useful part must be extracted. The most common example is a computer tape made by someone else, such as the Census Bureau or a Highway Department. In most cases, only a few items are desired for each geographical unit (such as a census tract) and the computer is used to extract it.

Frequently the data, once extracted, are at too fine a level of detail to be useful. They might come for city blocks or traffic zones or individual people or households. The computer is very helpful in aggregating to a desired level, such as the census tract or the region.

After the data have been "sorted into the right boxes," a variety of problems arise regarding their format. The Census Bureau, for example, will usually provide marginal (single-dimension) distributions but not joints. Information about the structure of the joint distributions is available, and the computer does a fine job of matching these two sources to produce joint distributions. Another, more mundane job is simply collecting all the "final" data into a compact package that can be fed quickly into a computer simulation model.

Errors frequently creep into this collection and reduction process. It is thus desirable to be able to repeat the entire reduction sequence rapidly so that if an error is found "up stream," the entire data base can be readjusted quickly. We have developed an interrelated group of some 75 computer programs that enable us to reproduce the entire reduced data base for our simulation model from the raw data in a matter of one or two hours, depending upon where an error is detected.

Revealing Patterns

One of the problems in counting urban teeth is that there are a great number of them. It is sometimes difficult to see what the data are telling you. In response to this problem, we developed several fairly simple-minded instruments to reveal patterns.

The simplest of all is a shaded map. As a researcher begins to gain familiarity with a region, each location on a map creates a mental image and takes on a special meaning of its own. A two-dimensional map displaying, for example, percent minority or percent with a college education, can be a great aid to intuition. We have arranged things so that a researcher can get a great variety of such maps in any desired sequence while sitting at a time-shared computer console.

For others, a table is easier to understand than a map, particularly when many factors are involved at one time. For them, we have developed ways of relating, in tabular form, changes that are taking place with their causes. It is possible, for example, to ask: "What are the characteristics of the neighborhoods where the foreign-born are living, of the neighborhoods they are leaving, and of neighborhoods they are moving into?" Or, "What are the characteristics of neighborhoods that are permitting multiple-unit structures for the first time?"

Checking Honesty

As the researcher's understanding and intuition improve through observation of patterns in data and actual first-hand experiences, the natural tendency, be it conscious or subconscious, is to begin to formulate conceptual models (or theories) about what is taking place. One of the nice things about the computer is that it permits the user to express his or her theories in a wide variety of mathematical forms. The straight lines and smooth curves of earlier analyses are no longer necessary.

The computer also permits its user to relate lots of pieces of theory to each other in a meaningful whole which we are calling a simulation model. In this regard, it serves much the same function as a base for a clay model. If the raw clay can be thought of as the data and if the individual shapes of houses and trees and buildings and cars are the theories that gradually emerge under constant forming and reforming, then the board on which the individual pieces are mounted and gradually formed into a whole city is not unlike the computer. It serves as a collecting place where theories can be gathered and related to each other to form a whole.

A clay model must be checked visually against either photographs of the city or an actual view from a high building. A computer simulation, on the other hand, must be checked against more abstract data. Perhaps the best way to do this is to run the simulation from one known point in time to another and to see how well it predicts what actually took place during the intervening period.

This is not so simple as it might at first sound because, in any realistic simulation, the number of predictions is very large. Ours, for example, makes about 35,000 predictions for each simulated year. Once again, there exists a need to reveal patterns in this mass of numbers and hence reduce the overload problem. We have developed instruments that compare the model's results with actual data and suggest the cause of the errors between the two. The user can ask, for example, "What are the characteristics of neighborhoods into which too many old people moved (in the model)?" or "What are the characteristics of neighborhoods where builders (in the model) built too many rental units?"

We have also developed instruments that automatically interpret the errors and suggest changes in the model that will reduce them. We call these tuners. They are not so trustworthy as they might be, and require constant monitoring by a human operator.

In Conclusion

Taken together, the models and the instruments described in this Appendix provide a learning environment in which the student of urban change can quickly formulate theories and test them against reality. While the technical problems associated with developing some 200 compatible pieces are nontrivial, the concept is straightforward. It is not a familiar concept in many of the social sciences, but one that we feel takes good advantage of the increasing availability of data and computers and people who know how to use both.

Index

About the Authors

David Birch received the A.B. from Harvard College and the M.B.A. and D.B.A. from the Harvard University Graduate School of Business Administration, where he is now an associate professor. He also serves on the executive committee of the MIT-Harvard Joint Center for Urban Studies. He has been a consultant to the National Science Foundation, the Ford Foundation, the Oak Ridge National Laboratory, and the Houston/Galveston Area Council in Houston, Texas. He has been a research engineer at General Dynamics/Astronautics and at the California Institute of Technology's Jet Propulsion Laboratory. Dr. Birch is the author of a book, *The Businessman and the City* (Harvard Business School, 1967) and numerous articles and monographs on urban and regional growth.

Reilly Atkinson received the A.B. in physics from Harvard University and the Ph.D. in physics from Stanford University. He is presently a research associate at the Joint Center for Urban Studies in Cambridge, Massachusetts. Dr. Atkinson has also served as a senior urban scientist for the Boeing Company; as assistant professor of physics at Tufts University; and as research associate in physics at Washington University. He is the author of a number of articles which have appeared in physics journals.

Sven Sandström received the M.B.A. from the Stockholm School of Economics and the D.Sc. in civil engineering from the Royal Institute of Technology in Sweden, where he also worked as a planning consultant. While participating in the New Haven study, Dr. Sandström was a Ph.D. candidate in urban studies and planning at the Massachusetts Institute of Technology. He is presently a regional systems analyst with the International Bank for Reconstruction and Development in Washington, D.C.

Linda Stack received the B.A. from Wellesley College and is currently a graduate student at the Alfred P. Sloan School of Management at the Massachusetts Institute of Technology. She was a computer programmer on Project MAC at the Massachusetts Institute of Technology, and research assistant and chief programmer for the New Haven Simulation Project.